THE BEAUTIFUL IN MUSIC

The Library of Liberal Arts
OSKAR PIEST, FOUNDER

. . . .

THE BEAUTIFUL IN MUSIC

Eduard Hanslick

Translated by
Gustav Cohen

Edited, with an introduction, by
Morris Weitz

The Library of Liberal Arts
published by
THE BOBBS-MERRILL COMPANY, INC.
INDIANAPOLIS • NEW YORK

Eduard Hanslick: 1825 - 1904

THE BEAUTIFUL IN MUSIC was originally published in 1854

. . . .

COPYRIGHT ©, 1957

THE LIBERAL ARTS PRESS, INC.

A Division of

THE BOBBS MERRILL COMPANY, INC.

All Rights Reserved

Printed in the United States of America

Library of Congress Catalog Card Number: 57-14627

ISBN-0-672-60211-3 (pbk)

Seventh Printing

CONTENTS

EDITOR'S INTRODUCTION

I

It is a pleasure to welcome back the English translation of Eduard Hanslick's *Vom Musikalisch-Schönen*, which has been too long out of print. Written in 1854, when Hanslick was working as a government clerk in Vienna and doing part-time music criticism for the *Wiener Zeitung*, it has become a classic in musical aesthetics and, in my opinion, remains the best introduction to the subject. It is to music what Hume's *Inquiry Concerning Human Understanding* is to speculative philosophy, a devastating critique of unsupportable views and an attempt to state clearly and precisely the territories and boundaries of the areas they discuss. Because of its pervasive attack on the emotionalist and programmatic theories, its insistence upon music as sounds in their relations and not as depiction or narration, and its hardheaded analyses of basic concepts, *The Beautiful in Music* became an enormously read work, and increasingly so when the author's notoriety as the leading anti-Wagnerian of his generation grew. The book ran through nine German editions, an English one (1891), and French, Italian, and Russian editions as well.

The Beautiful in Music is only one of a dozen volumes published by Hanslick. Two others of these are autobiographical. He was born in Prague on September 11, 1825. His father lectured on philosophy and aesthetics at the *Hochschule* there and gave piano lessons. Fortune smiled on him to the extent of 40,000 guilder won in a lottery, which enabled him to marry one of his attractive students. Eduard was the second son of the marriage. Both parents guided him through his early experiences of music, opera, and literature. When he was nineteen, Hanslick entered the University of Prague to study law; in 1846 he went to Vienna to complete his fourth and final year.

Hanslick had previously met Richard Wagner in Marienbad in 1845 and in Dresden in 1846. The meetings were not successful, and both have written about them. The Wagner-Hanslick story is itself a fascinating one in the history of musical criticism and aesthetics; and indeed Hanslick is remembered by many people only as an infamous opponent of Wagner. The issue between them was fundamentally aesthetic and concerned the role of the music drama in the development of opera. Wagner championed his famous theory of opera as *Gesamtkunstwerk,* which Hanslick rejected because that implied a total dissolution of music. In their long controversy Hanslick never reduced his attack to the low and tactless level of Wagner who once, at a party to which Hanslick had been invited, read his early draft of *Die Meistersinger,* referring to Beckmesser, who later became the philistine, as Veit Hanslick. Hanslick sums up his case against Wagner in simple but piercing musical terms:

> What I have reproached him with is the violation of music by words, the unnaturalness and exaggeration of the expression, the annihilation of the singer and the art of singing by unvocal writing and orchestral din, the displacement of the melody of song by declamatory recitation, enervating monotony and measureless expansion, and finally, the unnatural, stilted progression of his diction, a diction which offends every feeling for fine speech.[1]

In 1848 Hanslick became music critic for the *Wiener Zeitung,* and thirteen years later was invited to become Professor of Music at the University of Vienna, where he gave what was probably the first music appreciation course in history. His influence on the musical life of Vienna was tremendous. He championed, among others, Mozart, Beethoven, and Brahms, the latter being his personal friend. His targets remained Wagner and other archromanticists—Bruckner, Liszt, and Berlioz. He died in Vienna on August 6, 1904.

1 Quoted in S. Deas, *In Defence of Hanslick* (London, 1940), p. 21.

II

The Beautiful in Music deals with the major problems of musical aesthetics: the aim of music, its intrinsic nature, the relation between music and reality, and the role of the listener. Throughout, Hanslick's main objective is the refutation of the popular and still-prevalent theory that feelings or emotions are the substance of musical sounds, and that the composer expresses his affective life in his music so that the listener shares in it. He denies that music is a language of the emotions or, by implication, of persons, places, things, events, or ideas. In the famous controversy between the autonomist and heteronomist views on the meaning of music, which has exercised musical and philosophical aesthetics for the last hundred years, he sides, therefore, with the autonomists.

The autonomist school holds that music is a self-sufficient realm of organized sounds which mean nothing. Hence music is no language of anything, including our emotions. Heteronomists, on the other hand, argue that music functions to denote or connote certain specific ideas, things, emotions, and consequently is a language in the sense of any ordinary language.

This conflict has raged from the days of Wagner and Hanslick and has been fanned by many musical aestheticians, including Gurney, Sullivan, and Pratt, among others. Philosophically, the basic issue has to do with the nature of language and meaning; and an examination of the arguments employed on both sides reveals, I think, a striking unanimity as to what language and meaning are. Language they take to be a system of signs which can be used by us to communicate in various ways. And meaning is conceived as the connotation or denotation of the signs in question. For both autonomists and heteronomists, music is a language and has meaning if and only if the musical sounds communicate certain references to listeners, where these references may be concepts or things (including emotions). When these sounds are like their references, they speak of music as "representing" nonmusical materials; and when they are unlike them, as "symbolizing" these materials.

"X means y to z," where "x" is a musical sound functioning as a sign, is equivalent to "x denotes or connotes y to z." To say, then, that music *is* a language, on this theory, is to say that music represents or symbolizes some concept or thing to some listener. The heteronomist argues that, since music is like or can be associated with all sorts of ideas and things, it is a language and has meaning. The autonomist counters that music is like nothing else (with the trivial exception of ono-matopoetic sounds) and cannot unarbitrarily be associated with anything; hence it is no language and means nothing.

Almost everyone considers Hanslick to be among the staunch-est advocates of the autonomous theory. After all, it was he who invented its famous slogan, "The essence of music is sound in motion." Further, he talks of music as arabesques or kaleidoscopes of sound. Again, he presents the most telling arguments against the programmatic and emotionalist versions of heteronomy. But all of this notwithstanding, I want to in-sist that Hanslick's total view on this matter adds up to a modified heteronomous theory, according to which musical sounds are like certain general features of human experience and, in this dimension, can be said to represent something nonmusical. In this sense music, for Hanslick, has a meaning and is a (restricted) language.

First, let us consider his argument against the extreme, emo-tionalist heteronomists, especially Wagner and his disciples. Music, for them, is a language of specific emotions, things, persons, ideas; it can be used to refer to and to describe any-thing. Hanslick says that music is incapable of such specific, concrete representation or symbolism because it simply has not the means as a medium for doing so. Without a specific vo-cabulary of fixed items, like words, nothing concrete can be communicated. To represent, to mean, to refer to anything specific by means of musical sounds, he says, is possible only if one could find a "causal nexus between these ideas and certain combinations of sound"; but this connection is simply not forthcoming. There is no fixed relationship between certain sounds and certain things (with the onomatopoetic exceptions) such that we could ever say that the one meant the other by being like it or by symbolizing it in any requisite uniform or nonarbitrary way. Take any instrumental composition, Hanslick suggests, and ask what particular feeling it supposedly depicts: "One will say 'love.' He may be right. Another thinks it is 'longing.' Perhaps so. A third feels it to be 'religious fervor.' Who can contradict him? Now, how can we talk of a definite feeling being *represented,* when nobody really knows *what* is represented?"

If music is not an embodiment of specific feelings, what then is it? Music is essentially certain tones in their harmonic and rhythmic relations. The art, the beauty of music consists in these sounds and not in their representational values. As sounds they are, Hanslick says, characterized by their strength, motion, and ratio, which give rise to intensity waxing and waning, to motion hastening and lingering, and to ingeniously complex and simple progression. And because of these musical characteristics certain aesthetic qualities present themselves in the sounds which we, the listeners, may describe as "graceful, gentle, violent, vigorous, elegant, fresh; all these ideas being expressible by corresponding modifications of sound." Thus, to say of a melody, for example, that it is graceful, is not to say that it represents or symbolizes anything graceful or even any feeling of gracefulness, if there be such, but rather that its lingering character, as sound, is graceful. It is graceful in the way, say, that a particular red may be said to be luscious or succulent. The gracefulness is presented in the sounds, it is not represented by them.

But consider specific emotions like love, fear, and anger. Although music cannot represent or symbolize these, Hanslick claims, it can represent—be like—certain pervasive features of our emotions. "*What* part of the feelings, then, can music represent, if not the subject involved in them? Only their *dynamic* properties. It may reproduce the motion accompanying psychical action, according to its momentum: speed, slowness, strength, weakness, increasing and decreasing intensity. But motion is only one of the concomitants of feeling,

not the feeling itself." Music cannot represent love, for example, but it can represent its dynamic element of movement,
its waxing or waning character, which it has in common with
all emotional states.

Hanslick, consequently, is a heteronomist in this limited
sense: music is a language of the dynamic properties of emotions and can be said to mean—i.e., to represent or to denote—
these properties. But, he adds, this linguistic feature is no
part of the beauty of music, which consists entirely of the
tones in their musical relationships.

Hanslick has other things to say in his book on the relation
between music and the natural world, the aims of composition, and the role of the listener. Always he rejects the view
that emotion is central. His discussion and justification of the
view that listening is a normative and not a descriptive problem, especially in Chapter V, is a brilliant defense of the
theory of contemplation—that listening to music ought to be a
painstaking attending to the unfolding of the tonal combinations, much more an intellectual and imaginative procedure
than an emotional one. The enjoyment or disappointment
derived from understanding the progression of sounds are the
only legitimate emotional accompaniments of proper musical
response.

III

Hanslick's writings have exerted much influence upon musical criticism and philosophical aesthetics. In musical criticism
for the most part, at least until recently, his critical assessments
of composers and their works have been rejected by many because of his bias against Wagner. For these he is pure anath-
ema. But recently other writers have turned to his evalua-
tions for what they take to be sound, lasting judgments of
musical compositions.

In aesthetics proper, Hanslick remains the force he always
was. Although many philosophers prefer to formulate his
central problem differently, especially in regard to meaning
and language, where the relational, correspondence theories

have been repudiated, they still recognize the clarity and force of his way of putting the problem of meaning in music and the credibility of his solution. For them, Hanslick's *The Beautiful in Music* remains a model of aesthetic analysis and philosophy.

MORRIS WEITZ

SELECTED BIBLIOGRAPHY

WORKS OF EDUARD HANSLICK

Vom Musikalisch-Schönen. Leipzig, 1854; 7th ed., 1885. (*The Beautiful in Music.* Tr. Gustav Cohen. London, 1891.)
Geschichte des Concertwesens in Wien. 2 vols. Vienna, 1869-70.
Die moderne Oper. 9 vols. Berlin, 1875-1900.
Suite: Aufsätze über Musik und Musiker. Vienna, 1885.
Concerte, Componisten und Virtuosen der letzten 15 Jahre. Berlin, 1886.
Aus meinem Leben. 2 vols. Berlin, 1894.

COLLATERAL READING

Deas, Stewart. *In Defence of Hanslick.* London, 1940.
Pleasants, Henry (ed.). *Vienna's Golden Years, 1850-1900.* New York, 1950.

TRANSLATOR'S PREFACE

If I have ventured to translate Dr. Eduard Hanslick's *Vom Musikalisch-Schönen,* I have done so with a full knowledge of the shortcomings which every translation must present, and especially one like this, the original of which is so inimitable in style and so thoroughly German in construction that even far more competent writers than myself would find it difficult, if not impossible, to do complete justice to it. My excuse for undertaking so arduous a task must be the desire to introduce to the English reader one of the most remarkable books on musical aesthetics, and one which has deservedly gained a wide reputation among the German-speaking communities. The work is not of recent date, the first edition having appeared close on forty years ago; yet, as is the case with all works dealing with principles and not with questions of local or contemporary interest, the fact of its age in no way detracts from its importance. In conclusion, I may say that I have not aimed so much at perfection in style as at reflecting with fidelity the mind and spirit of the author.

GUSTAV COHEN

Sale, May, 1891.

NOTE ON THE TEXT

The present edition of Eduard Hanslick's *The Beautiful in Music* is the Gustav Cohen translation of the seventh German edition first published in 1891. Minor corrections have been made in the translation, and spelling and punctuation have been modified to conform with preferred American usage.

The Beautiful in Music

PREFACE TO THE SEVENTH EDITION

This, the seventh edition of the work which first appeared in the year 1854, does not differ materially from the fifth (1876) and sixth (1881) editions, but merely contains some explanatory and amplifying additions. By way of introducing it to the public I should best like to borrow the words with which the estimable Fr. Th. Vischer has just prefaced the reprint of an older essay of his ("Der Traum").[1] "I include this essay," says Vischer, "in the present series, without shielding it from the attacks which have been leveled against it. I have also refrained from improving it by retouches, excepting a few unimportant alterations. I might now, perhaps, here and there choose a different mode of expression, give a fuller exposition, or assert things in a more qualified and guarded manner. Who is ever completely satisfied with a work which he reads again after the lapse of years? Yet we know but too well that corrective touches often rather spoil than improve."

If I were to enter upon a polemic campaign and reply to all criticisms which my book has provoked, this volume would grow to an alarming size. My convictions have remained unaltered, and so has the irreconcilable antagonism of the contrary musical parties of the present day.[2] The reader will, therefore, no doubt allow me to repeat some of the remarks which I made in the preface to the third edition. I know the shortcomings of this essay but too well; still, the favorable re-

[1] *Altes und Neues* (Stuttgart, 1881), p. 187.

[2] O. Hostinsky's interesting and carefully worded essay ("Das Musikalische-Schöne und das Gesammtkunstwerk vom Standpunkt der formalen Aesthetik," Leipzig, 1877) is a paradoxical exception. Though in the first part he, to all appearance, clearly and fully endorses my premises, he subsequently, in discussing the term *Kunstverein* (the combination of arts), narrows, twists, and interprets them in such a manner as to reach conclusions completely at variance with my own.

3

ception accorded to the earlier editions—a reception which far exceeded my expectations—and the highly gratifying interest taken in the book by eminent experts, proficient both as philosophers and musicians, have convinced me that my views— the somewhat categorical and rhapsodical manner in which they were originally stated notwithstanding—have fallen on fertile ground. A very notable concurrence with these views I found, to my agreeable surprise, in the aphorisms and short essays on music by Grillparzer, published only some ten years ago, after the poet's death. Some of the most valuable of his propositions I could not refrain from quoting in this new edition, while in my essay, "Grillparzer und die Musik," I have discussed them at greater length.[3]

Certain vehement opponents of mine have occasionally imputed to me a flat and unqualified denial of whatever goes under the name of feeling, but every dispassionate and attentive reader will have readily observed that I only protest against the intrusion of the feelings upon the province of science; in other words, that I take up the cudgels against those aesthetic enthusiasts who, though presuming to teach the musician, in reality only dilate upon their own tinkling opium dreams. I am quite at one with those who hold that the ultimate worth of the beautiful must ever depend upon the immediate verdict of the feelings. But at the same time I firmly adhere to the conviction that all the customary appeals to our emotional faculty can never show the way to a single musical law.

This conviction forms one of the propositions—the principal but negative proposition—of this inquiry, which is mainly and primarily directed against the widely accepted doctrine that the office of music is "to represent feelings." It is difficult to see why this should be thought equivalent to "affirming that music is absolutely destitute of feeling." The rose smells sweet, yet its subject is surely not the representation of the odor; the forest is cool and shady, but it certainly does not represent "the feeling of coolness and shadiness." It is not a mere

3 *Musikalische Stationen* (Berlin, 1878), p. 331, etc.

verbal quibble if the term "to represent" is here expressly
taken exception to, for it is this term which is answerable for
the grossest errors in musical aesthetics. The "representing"
of something always involves the conception of two separate
and distinct objects which by a special act are purposely
brought into relation with each other.

Emanuel Geibel, by a felicitously chosen parallel, has described this relation in the following distichs with greater
perspicuity and more agreeably than philosophic analyses
could ever do:

> *Warum glückt es dir nie, Musik mit Worten zu schil-*
> *dern?*
> *Weil sie, ein rein Element, Bild und Gedanken ver-*
> *schmäht.*
> *Selbst das Gefühl ist nur wie ein sanft durchschei-*
> *nender Flussgrund,*
> *Drauf ihr klingender Strom sinkend und schwellend*
> *entrollt.*

Now, as I have reason to believe that the author of these
beautiful lines was inspired by thoughts which this essay suggested, it appears to me that my views, so vigorously denounced
by romantic enthusiasts, are, after all, quite compatible with
true poetry.

The negative proposition referred to is complemented by
its correlative, the affirmative proposition: the beauty of a
composition is *specifically musical,* i.e., it inheres in the combinations of musical sounds and is independent of all alien,
extramusical notions. The author has honestly endeavored to
make an exhaustive inquiry into the positive aspects of the
"musically beautiful," upon which the very existence of our
art and the supreme laws of its aesthetics depend. If, nevertheless, the controversial and negative elements predominate,
I must plead the circumstances of the time as my excuse. When
I wrote this treatise the advocates of the "music of the future"
were loudest in their praises of it, and could but provoke a
reaction on the part of people holding opinions such as I do.
Just when I was busy preparing the second edition, Liszt's

"Program Symphonies" appeared, which denied to music more completely than ever before its independent sphere and dosed the listener with a sort of vision-promoting medicine. Since then, the world has been enriched by Richard Wagner's *Tristan, Nibelungen Ring,* and his doctrine of the "infinite melody," i.e., formlessness exalted into a principle—the intoxicating effect of opium manifested both in vocal and instrumental music, for the worship of which a temple has been specially erected at Bayreuth.

I trust I may be pardoned if in view of such symptoms I felt no inclination to abbreviate or temper the polemic part of this essay but pointed, on the contrary, more emphatically than ever to the one immutable factor in music, *purely musical beauty,* such as our great masters have embodied in their works, and such as true musical genius will produce to the end of time.

EDUARD HANSLICK

Vienna, January, 1885.

CHAPTER I

AESTHETICS AS FOUNDED ON FEELINGS

The course hitherto pursued in musical aesthetics has nearly always been hampered by the false assumption that the object was not so much to inquire into what is beautiful in music as to describe the feelings which music awakens. This view entirely coincides with that of the older systems of aesthetics, which considered the beautiful solely in reference to the sensations aroused and the philosophy of beauty as the offspring of sensation (αἴσθησις).

Such systems of aesthetics are not only unphilosophical, but they assume an almost sentimental character when applied to the most ethereal of all arts; and though no doubt pleasing to a certain class of enthusiasts, they afford but little enlightenment to a thoughtful student who, in order to learn something about the real nature of music, will, above all, remain deaf to the fitful promptings of passion and not, as most manuals on music direct, turn to the emotions as a source of knowledge.

The tendency in science to study as far as possible the objective aspect of things could not but affect researches into the nature of beauty. A satisfactory result, however, is only to be attained by relinquishing a method which starts from subjective sensation only to bring us face to face with it once more after taking us for a poetic ramble over the surface of the subject. Any such investigation will prove utterly futile unless the method obtaining in natural science be followed, at least in the sense of dealing with the things themselves, in order to determine what is permanent and objective in them when dissociated from the ever-varying impressions which they produce.

Poetry, sculpture, and painting are, in point of well-

7

metaphysics thrown out

grounded aesthetic treatment, far in advance of music. Few writers on these subjects still labor under the delusion that from a general metaphysical conception of beauty (a conception which necessarily varies with the art) the aesthetic principles of any specific art can be deduced. Formerly, the aesthetic principles of the various arts were supposed to be governed by some supreme metaphysical principle of general aesthetics. Now, however, the conviction is daily growing that each individual art can be understood only by studying its technical limits and its inherent nature. "Systems" are gradually being supplanted by "researches" founded on the thesis that the laws of beauty for each art are inseparably associated with the individuality of the art and the nature of its medium.[1]

In the aesthetics of rhetoric, sculpture, and painting, no less than in art criticism—the practical application of the foregoing sciences—the rule has already been laid down that aesthetic investigations must above all consider the beautiful object, and not the perceiving subject.

Music alone is unable, apparently, to adopt this objective mode of procedure. Rigidly distinguishing between its theoretico-grammatical rules and its aesthetic researches, men generally state the former in extremely dry and prosaic language, while they wrap the latter in a cloud of high-flown sentimen-

[1] Robert Schumann has done a great deal of mischief by his proposition (*Collected Works*, I, 43): "The aesthetic principles of one art are those of the others, the material alone being different." Grillparzer expresses a very different opinion and takes the right view when he says (*Complete Works*, IX, 142): "Probably no worse service has ever been rendered to the arts than when German writers included them all in the collective name of art. Many points they undoubtedly have in common, yet they diverge widely not only in the means they employ, but also in their fundamental principles. The essential difference between music and poetry might be brought into strong relief by showing that music primarily affects the senses and, after rousing the emotions, reaches the intellect last of all. Poetry, on the other hand, first raises up an idea which in its turn excites the emotions, while it affects the senses only as an extreme result of its highest or lowest form. They, therefore, pursue an exactly opposite course, for one spiritualizes the material, whereas the other materializes the spiritual."

tality. The task of clearly realizing music as a self-subsistent form of the beautiful has hitherto presented insurmountable difficulties to musical aesthetics, and the dictates of "emotion" still haunt their domain in broad daylight. Beauty in music is still as much as ever viewed only in connection with its subjective impressions, and books, critiques, and conversations continually remind us that the emotions are the only aesthetic foundations of music, and that they alone are warranted in defining its scope.

Music, we are told, cannot, like poetry, entertain the mind with definite conceptions; nor yet the eye, like sculpture and painting, with visible forms. Hence, it is argued, its object must be to work on the feelings. "Music has to do with feelings." This expression, "has to do," is highly characteristic of all works on musical aesthetics. But what the nature of the link is that connects music with the emotions, or certain pieces of music with certain emotions; by what laws of nature it is governed; what the canons of art are that determine its form —all these questions are left in complete darkness by the very people who have "to do" with them. Only when one's eyes have become somewhat accustomed to this obscurity does it become manifest that the emotions play a double part in music, as currently understood.

On the one hand it is said that the aim and object of music is to excite emotions, i.e., pleasurable emotions; on the other hand, the emotions are said to be the subject matter which musical works are intended to illustrate.

Both propositions are alike in this, that one is as false as the other.

The refutation of the first of these propositions, which forms the introduction to most manuals of music, must not detain us long. The beautiful, strictly speaking, aims at nothing, since it is nothing but a form which, though available for many purposes according to its nature, has, as such, no aim beyond itself. If the contemplation of something beautiful arouses pleasurable feelings, this effect is distinct from the beautiful as such. I may, indeed, place a beautiful object before an observer with the avowed purpose of giving him pleasure, but this purpose in no way affects the beauty of the object. The beautiful is and remains beautiful though it arouse no emotion whatever, and though there be no one to look at it. In other words, although the beautiful exists for the gratification of an observer, it is independent of him.

In this sense music, too, has no aim (object), and the mere fact that this particular art is so closely bound up with our feelings by no means justifies the assumption that its aesthetic principles depend on this union.

In order to examine this relation critically we must, in the first place, scrupulously distinguish between the terms "feeling" and "sensation," although in ordinary parlance no objection need be raised to their indiscriminate use.

"Sensation" is the act of perceiving some sensible quality such as a sound or a color, whereas "feeling" is the consciousness of some psychical activity, i.e., a state of satisfaction or discomfort.

If I note (perceive) with my senses the odor or taste of some object, or its form, color, or sound, I call this state of consciousness "my sensation" of these qualities; but if sadness, hope, cheerfulness, or hatred appreciably raise me above or depress me below the habitual level of mental activity, I am said to "feel." [2]

The beautiful, first of all, affects our senses. This, however, is not peculiar to the beautiful alone, but is common to all phenomena whatsoever. Sensation, the beginning and condition of all aesthetic enjoyment, is the source of feeling in its widest sense, and this fact presupposes some relation, and often a highly complex one, between the two. No art is required to produce a sensation; a single sound or color may suffice. As previously stated, the two terms are generally employed promiscuously; but older writers speak of "sensation" where we

[2] Older philosophers agree with modern physiologists in the definition of these terms, and I unhesitatingly prefer this definition to the terminology of Hegel's school of philosophy, which, as is well known, distinguishes between internal and external sensations.

should use the term "feeling." What those writers intend to convey, therefore, is that the object of music is to arouse our feelings, and to fill our hearts with piety, love, joy, or sadness.

In point of fact, however, this is the aim neither of music nor of any other art. An art aims, above all, at producing something beautiful which affects not our feelings but the organ of pure contemplation, our *imagination*.[3]

It is rather curious that musicians and the older writers on aesthetics take into account only the contrast of "feeling" and "intellect," quite oblivious of the fact that the main point at issue lies halfway between the horns of this supposed dilemma. A musical composition originates in the composer's imagination and is intended for the imagination of the listener. Our imagination, it is true, does not merely contemplate the beautiful, but contemplates it with intelligence—the object being, as it were, mentally inspected and criticized. Our judgment, however, is formed so rapidly that we are unconscious of the separate acts involved in the process, whence the delusion arises that what in reality depends upon a complex train of reasoning is merely an act of intuition.

The word *Anschauung* (viewing, contemplating) is no longer applied to visual processes only but also to the functions of the other senses. It is, in fact, eminently suited to describe the act of attentive hearing, which is nothing but a mental inspection of a succession of musical images. Our imagination, withal, is not an isolated faculty, for though the vital spark originates in the senses, it forthwith kindles the flame of the intellect and the emotions. A true conception of the beautiful is, nevertheless, independent of this aspect of the question.

In the pure act of listening we enjoy the music alone and

[3] Hegel has shown that the method of examining into the "sensations" (i.e., "feelings" according to our terminology) which a work of art awakens proceeds on indefinite lines and ignores the truly concrete element altogether. "What we are sensible of," he says, "is indissolubly connected with the most abstract and individual subjectivity. The several kinds of sensations produced are, therefore, different in a subjective sense only and not distinct modes of the thing itself." (*Aesthetik*, I, 142.)

do not think of importing into it any extraneous matter. But the tendency to allow our feelings to be aroused implies something extraneous to the music. An exclusive activity of the intellect, resulting from the contemplation of the beautiful, involves not an aesthetic but a *logical* relation, while a predominant action of the feelings brings us onto still more slippery ground, implying, as it does, a *pathological* relation.

These inferences, drawn long ago from principles of general aesthetics, apply with equal force to the beautiful in every art. If music, therefore, is to be treated as an art, it is not our feelings but our imagination which must supply the aesthetic tests. It is as well to make this premise hypothetical, seeing that the soothing effect of music on the human passions is always affirmed with such emphasis that we are often in doubt whether music is a police regulation, an educational rule, or a medical prescription.

Yet musicians are less prone to believe that all arts must be uniformly gauged by our feelings than that this principle is true of music alone. It is this very power and tendency of music to arouse in the listener any given emotion which, they think, distinguishes this art from all the others.[4]

As on a previous occasion we were unable to accept the doctrine that it is the aim of art in general to produce any such effect, we are now equally unable to regard it as the specific aim of music to do so. Grant that the true organ with which the beautiful is apprehended is the imagination, and it follows that all arts are likely to affect the feelings indirectly. Are we not moved by a great historical picture with the vividness of actual experience? Do not Raphael's Madonnas fill us with piety, and do not Poussin's landscapes awaken in us an irresist-

4 At a time when no distinction was made even between "feeling" and "sensation," a more critical examination into the varieties of the former was, of course, out of the question. Sensuous and intellectual feelings, the enduring state known as "frame of mind," the acute or emotional state, inclination and passion, no less than the gradations peculiar to the latter, the *pathos* of the Greeks and the *passio* of the more modern Romans, were all confounded in one inextricable jumble, while of music nothing was predicated except that it was the art of exciting emotions.

ible desire to roam about in the world? Do our feelings remain callous to a sight such as the Strasbourg Cathedral? All these questions admit of but one reply, which is equally true of poetry and of many extra-aesthetic states of mind such as religious fervor, eloquence, etc. We thus see that all other arts, too, affect us with considerable force. The inherent peculiarities assumed to distinguish music from the other arts would depend, therefore, upon the degree of intensity of this force. The attempt, however, thus to solve the problem is not only highly unscientific but is, moreover, of no avail, because the decision whether one is more deeply affected by a symphony by Mozart, a tragedy by Shakespeare, a poem by Uhland, or a rondo by Hummel must depend, after all, on the individual himself. Those again who hold that music affects our feelings "directly," whereas the other arts do so only through the medium of ideas, express the same error in other words. For we *Schopenhauer* have already seen that the excitation of feelings by the beautiful in music is but one of its indirect effects, our imagination only being directly affected. Musical dissertations constantly recall the analogy which undoubtedly exists between music and architecture, but what architect in his senses ever conceived the *aim* of architecture to be the excitation of feelings, or the feelings the subject matter of his art?

Every real work of art appeals to our emotional faculty in some way, but none in any exclusive way. No canon peculiar to musical aesthetics only can be deduced from the fact that there is a certain connection between music and the emotions. We might as well study the properties of wine by getting drunk. The crux of the question is the specific mode in which music affects our feelings. Hence, instead of enlarging on the vague and secondary effects of musical phenomena, we ought to endeavor to penetrate deeply into the spirit of the works themselves and to explain their effects by the laws of their inherent nature. A poet or painter would hardly persuade himself that when he has ascertained the "feelings" his landscape or drama awakens, he has obtained a rationale of the beauties contained in it. He will seek to discover the source of the irresistible power which makes us enjoy the work in this particular form and in no other. Writers on this subject are by no means justified in confusing emotional impressions and musical beauty (instead of adopting the scientific method of keeping these two factors apart as much as possible) simply because an inquiry of this kind offers in respect of music, as we shall presently see, far greater difficulties than any other art, and because such an inquiry cannot go below a certain depth.

Independently of the fact that our feelings can never become the basis of aesthetic laws, there are many cogent reasons why we should not trust to the feelings aroused by music. As a consequence of our mental constitution, words, titles, and other conventional associations (in sacred, military, and operatic music more especially) give to our feelings and thoughts a direction which we often falsely ascribe to the character of the music itself. For, in reality, there is no causal nexus between a musical composition and the feelings it may excite, as the latter vary with our experience and impressibility. The present generation often wonder how their forefathers could imagine that just this arrangement of sounds adequately represented just this feeling. We need but instance the effects which works by Mozart, Beethoven, and Weber produced when they were new as compared with their effects on us. How many compositions by Mozart were thought by his contemporaries to be the most perfect expressions of passion, warmth, and vigor of which music is capable! The placidity and moral sunshine of Haydn's symphonies were placed in contrast with the violent bursts of passion, the internal strife, the bitter and acute grief embodied in Mozart's music.[5] Twenty or thirty years later, precisely the same comparison was made between Beethoven and Mozart. Mozart, the emblem

---

[5] Of Rochlitz in particular there are sayings on record about Mozart's instrumental music which sound rather strange to our ears. This same Rochlitz describes the graceful *minuet-capriccio* in Weber's "Sonata in A flat" as "the copious, incessant effusion of a passionate and fiercely agitated mind, controlled, withal, by a marvelous steadiness of purpose."

of supreme and transcendent passion, was replaced by Beethoven, while he himself was promoted to the Olympic classicality of Haydn. Every observant musician will, in the course of his own life, experience analogous changes of taste. The musical merit of the many compositions which at one time made so deep an impression, and the aesthetic enjoyment which their originality and beauty still yield, are not altered in the least by this dissimilar effect on the feelings at different periods. Thus, there is no invariable and inevitable nexus between musical works and certain states of mind; the connection being, on the contrary, of a far more transient kind than in any other art.

It is manifest, therefore, that the effect of music on the emotions does not possess the attributes of inevitableness, exclusiveness, and uniformity that a phenomenon from which aesthetic principles are to be deduced ought to have.

Far be it from us to underrate the deep emotions which music awakens from their slumber, or the feelings of joy or sadness which our minds dreamily experience. It is one of the most precious and inestimable secrets of nature that an art should have the power of evoking feelings entirely free from worldly associations and kindled, as it were, by the spark divine. It is only the unscientific procedure of deducing aesthetic principles from such facts against which we protest. Music may, undoubtedly, awaken feelings of great joy or intense sorrow; but might not the same or a still greater effect be produced by the news that we have won the first prize in the lottery, or by the dangerous illness of a friend? So long as we refuse to include lottery tickets among the symphonies, or medical bulletins among the overtures, we must refrain from treating the emotions as an aesthetic monopoly of music in general or a certain piece of music in particular. Everything depends upon the specific *modus operandi* by means of which music evokes such feelings. The fourth and fifth chapters will be devoted to a critical examination of the influence which music exerts on our feelings, and we shall then have occasion to consider the positive aspect of this remarkable connection.

In this, the introductory chapter of our work, our object was to shed as much light as possible on its negative aspect as a standing protest against an unscientific principle.

Herbart (in the ninth chapter of his *Encyclopaedia*), to the best of my knowledge, struck the first blow at the theory that the feelings are the foundation of musical aesthetics. After expressing his disapproval of the vague manner in which works of art are criticized, he goes on to say:

> Interpreters of dreams and astrologers have for thousands of years persistently ignored the fact that people dream because they are asleep, and that the stars appear now in one part of the heavens and now in another because they are in motion. Similarly, there are even good musicians who still cling to the belief that music is capable of expressing definite feelings, as though the feelings which it accidentally arouses, and to express which music may for this very reason be employed, were the proximate cause of the rules of simple and double counterpoint. For these alone form the groundwork of music. What subject, we might ask, did the old masters mean to illustrate when they developed all the possible forms of the fugue? No subject at all. Their thoughts did not travel beyond the limits of the art, but penetrated deeply into its inmost recesses. He who adheres to meanings thereby betrays his dislike of the inner aspect of things and his love of mere outward appearance.

It is much to be regretted that Herbart refrained from prosecuting these occasional strictures in more detail, and that along with these brilliant flashes there go some rather questionable statements; at all events, we shall presently see that the views we have just quoted failed to gain the regard they so well merited.

NOTE. Our present purpose, we think, hardly makes it incumbent on us to mention the authors of the doctrines which it is our object to disprove, these doctrines being not so much the fruit of original speculation as the enunciation of traditional convictions that have gained great popularity. To show how deeply these doctrines have taken root, we will select some examples from their vast number. The following emanate from the pens both of old and modern writers on music.

Mattheson: "When composing a melody, our chief aim should be to illustrate a certain emotion (if not more than one)." (*Vollkommener Capellmeister*, p. 143.)

Neidhardt: "The ultimate aim of music is to rouse all the passions by means of sound and rhythm, rivaling the most eloquent oration." (Preface to *Temperatur*.)

J. N. Forkel understands "figures in music" in the same sense as in poetry or rhetoric—namely, "as the expression of the various modes in which sensations and emotions gain utterance." (*Über die Theorie der Musik*, Göttingen, 1777, p. 26.)

J. Mosel defines music as "the art of expressing certain emotions through the medium of systematically combined sounds."

C. F. Michaelis: "Music is the art of expressing sensations by modulated sounds. It is the language of emotion," etc. (*Über den Geist der Tonkunst*, 2nd essay, 1800, p. 29.)

Marpurg: "The composer's task is to copy nature . . . to stir the passions at will . . . to express the living movements of the soul and the cravings of the heart." (*Krit. Musikus*, Vol. I, 1750, § 40.)

W. Heinse: "To picture, or rather to rouse the passions is the chief and final aim of music." (*Musikal. Dialoge*, 1805, p. 30.)

J. J. Engel: "A symphony, a sonata, etc., must be the representation of some passion developed in a variety of forms." (*Über musik. Malerei*, 1780, p. 29.)

J. Ph. Kirnberger: "A melodious phrase (theme) is a phrase taken from the language of emotion. It induces in a sensitive listener the same state of mind which gave birth to it." (*Kunst des reinen Satzes*, Part II, p. 152.)

Pierer's *Universallexicon* (2nd ed.): "Music is the art of expressing sensations and states of mind by means of pleasing sounds. It is superior to poetry because the latter can only (!)

describe emotions which the intellect apprehends, whereas music expresses vague and undefinable emotions and sensations."

G. Schilling's *Universallexicon der Tonkunst* gives a similar explanation under the heading "Musik."

Koch defines music as "the art of suggesting trains of pleasurable feelings through the medium of sound."

A. André: "Music is the art of producing sounds capable of expressing, exciting, and sustaining feelings and passions." (*Lehrbuch der Tonkunst,* I.)

Sulzer: "While language expresses our feelings in words, music expresses them by sounds." (*Theorie der schönen Künste.*)

J. W. Boehm: "Not to the intellect do the sweet strains of music appeal, but to our emotional faculty only." (*Analyse des Schönen der Musik,* Vienna, 1830, p. 62.)

Gottfried Weber: "Music is the art of expressing emotions through the medium of sound." (*Theorie der Tonsetzkunst,* I [2nd ed.], 15.)

F. Hand: "Music represents emotions. Each feeling and each state of mind has its own inherent sound and rhythm, and these have their objective counterpart in music." (*Aesthetik der Tonkunst,* I [1837], § 24.)

Amadeus Autodidaktus: "Music has its origin and its roots in the world of sentiment and sensation. Musically melodious sounds (!) are a sealed book to the intellect, which only describes and analyzes sensations. . . . They appeal to the feelings," etc. (*Aphorismen über Musik,* Leipzig, 1847, p. 329.)

Fermo Bellini: "Music is the art of expressing sentiments and passions through the medium of sound." (*Manuale di Musica,* Milano, Ricordi, 1853.)

Friedrich Thiersch: "Music is the art of expressing, and of exciting feelings and emotions by groups of selected sounds." (*Allgemeine Aesthetik,* Berlin, 1846, § 18, p. 101.)

A. v. Dommer: "The object of music: music is to awaken our feelings, and these, in their turn, are to raise up images in the mind." (*Elemente der Musik,* Leipzig, 1862, p. 174.)

Richard Wagner: *Das Kunstwerk der Zukunft (Selected Works,* III, [1850] 99—similar passages occurring in his other writings). "The organ of the emotions is sound; its intentionally aesthetic language is music." In Wagner's later writings his definitions become still more obscure, music being there for him "the art of expression in the abstract" ("Oper und Drama," *Coll. Writings,* III, 343) which, as a "conception of the universe," he deems capable of "comprehending the essence of things in its immediate manifestation," etc. ("Beethoven," 1870, p. 6, etc.)

CHAPTER II

DOES MUSIC REPRESENT FEELINGS?

The proposition that the feelings are the subject which music has to represent is due partly to the theory according to which the ultimate aim of music is to excite feelings and partly to an amended form of this theory.

A philosophical disquisition into an art demands a clear definition of its subject matter. The diversity of the subject matter of the various arts and the fundamental difference in the mode of treatment are a natural sequence of the dissimilarity of the senses to which they severally appeal. Every art comprises a range of ideas which it expresses after its own fashion in sound, language, color, stone, etc. A work of art, therefore, endows a definite conception with a material form of beauty. This definite conception, its embodiment, and the union of both are the conditions of an aesthetic ideal with which a critical examination into every art is indissolubly connected.

The subject of a poem, a painting, or a statue may be expressed in words and reduced to ideas. We say, for instance, this picture represents a flower girl, this statue a gladiator, this poem one of Roland's exploits. Upon the more or less perfect embodiment of the particular subject in the artist's production depends our verdict respecting the beauty of the work of art.

The whole gamut of human feelings has with almost complete unanimity been proclaimed to be the subject of music, since the emotions were thought to be in antithesis to the definiteness of intellectual conceptions. This was supposed to be the feature by which the musical ideal is distinguished from the ideal of the other fine arts and poetry. According to

20

this theory, therefore, sound and its ingenious combinations are but the material and the medium of expression by which the composer represents love, courage, piety, and delight. The innumerable varieties of emotion constitute the idea which, on being translated into sound, assumes the form of a musical composition. The beautiful melody and the skillful harmony as such do not charm us, but only what they imply: the whispering of love, or the clamor of ardent combatants.

In order to escape from such vague notions we must, first of all, sever from their habitual associations metaphors of the above description. The *whispering* may be expressed, true, but not the whispering of love; the *clamor* may be reproduced, undoubtedly, but not the clamor of ardent combatants. Music may reproduce phenomena such as whispering, storming, roaring, but the feelings of love or anger have only a subjective existence.

Definite feelings and emotions are unsusceptible of being embodied in music.

Our emotions have no isolated existence in the mind and cannot, therefore, be evoked by an art which is incapable of representing the remaining series of mental states. They are, on the contrary, dependent on physiological and pathological conditions, on notions and judgments—in fact, on all the processes of human reasoning which so many conceive as antithetical to the emotions.

What, then, transforms an indefinite feeling into a definite one—into the feeling of longing, hope, or love? Is it the mere degree of intensity, the fluctuating rate of inner motion? Assuredly not. The latter may be the same in the case of dissimilar feelings or may, in the case of the same feeling, vary with the time and the person. Only by virtue of ideas and judgments—unconscious though we may be of them when our feelings run high—can an indefinite state of mind pass into a definite feeling. The feeling of hope is inseparable from the conception of a happier state which is to come, and which we compare with the actual state. The feeling of sadness involves the notion of a past state of happiness. These are perfectly definite ideas or conceptions, and in default of them—the apparatus of thought, as it were—no feeling can be called "hope" or "sadness," for through them alone can a feeling assume a definite character. On excluding these conceptions from consciousness, nothing remains but a vague sense of motion which at best could not rise above a general feeling of satisfaction or discomfort. The feeling of love cannot be conceived apart from the image of the beloved being, or apart from the desire and the longing for the possession of the object of our affections. It is not the kind of psychical activity but the intellectual substratum, the subject underlying it, which constitutes it love. Dynamically speaking, love may be gentle or impetuous, buoyant or depressed, and yet it remains love. This reflection alone ought to make it clear that music can express only those qualifying adjectives, and not the substantive, love, itself. A determinate feeling (a passion, an emotion) as such never exists without a definable meaning which can, of course, only be communicated through the medium of definite ideas. Now, since music as an "indefinite form of speech" is admittedly incapable of expressing definite ideas, is it not a psychologically unavoidable conclusion that it is likewise incapable of expressing definite emotions? For the definite character of an emotion rests entirely on the meaning involved in it.

How it is that music may, nevertheless, awaken feelings (though not necessarily so) such as sadness and joy we shall try to explain hereafter when we come to examine music from a subjective point of view. At this stage of our inquiry it is enough to determine whether music is capable of representing any definite emotion whatever. To this question only a negative answer can be given, the definiteness of an emotion being inseparably connected with concrete notions and conceptions, and to reduce these to a material form is altogether beyond the power of music. A certain class of ideas, however, is quite susceptible of being adequately expressed by means which unquestionably belong to the sphere of music proper. This class comprises all ideas which, consistently with the organ to which they appeal, are associated with audible changes of strength, motion, and ratio: the ideas of intensity waxing and diminishing; of motion hastening and lingering; of ingeniously complex and simple progression, etc. The aesthetic expression of music may be described by terms such as graceful, gentle, violent, vigorous, elegant, fresh—all these ideas being expressible by corresponding modifications of sound. We may, therefore, use those adjectives as directly describing musical phenomena without thinking of the ethical meanings attaching to them in a psychological sense, and which, from the habit of associating ideas, we readily ascribe to the effect of the music, or even mistake for purely musical properties.

The ideas which a composer expresses are mainly and primarily of a purely musical nature. His imagination conceives a definite and graceful melody aiming at nothing beyond itself. Every concrete phenomenon suggests the class to which it belongs or some still wider conception in which the latter is included, and by continuing this process the idea of the absolute is reached at last. This is true also of musical phenomena. This melodious adagio, for instance, softly dying away, suggests the ideas of gentleness and concord in the abstract. Our imaginative faculty, ever ready to establish relations between the conceptions of art and our sentiments, may construe these softly ebbing strains of music in a still loftier sense, e.g., as the placid resignation of a mind at peace with itself; and they may rouse even a vague sense of everlasting rest.

The primary aim of poetry, sculpture, and painting is likewise to produce some concrete image. Only by way of inference can the picture of a flower girl call up the wider notion of maidenly content and modesty, the picture of a snow-covered churchyard the transitoriness of earthly existence. In like manner, but far more vaguely and capriciously, may the listener discover in a piece of music the idea of youthful contentedness or that of transitoriness. These abstract notions, however, are by no means the subject matter of the pictures or the musical compositions, and it is still more absurd to talk as if the feelings of "transitoriness" or of "youthful contentedness" could be represented by them.

There are ideas which, though not occurring as feelings, are yet capable of being fully expressed by music; and conversely, there are feelings which affect our minds but which are so constituted as to defy their adequate expression by any ideas which music can represent.

What part of the feelings, then, can music represent, if not the subject involved in them?

Only their dynamic properties. It may reproduce the motion accompanying psychical action, according to its momentum: speed, slowness, strength, weakness, increasing and decreasing intensity. But motion is only one of the concomitants of feeling, not the feeling itself. It is a popular fallacy to suppose that the descriptive power of music is sufficiently qualified by saying that, although incapable of representing the subject of a feeling, it may represent the feeling itself—not the object of love, but the feeling of love. In reality, however, music can do neither. It cannot reproduce the feeling of love but only the element of motion; and this may occur in any other feeling just as well as in love, and in no case is it the distinctive feature. The term "love" is as abstract as "virtue" or "immortality," and it is quite superfluous to assure us that music is unable to express abstract notions. No art can do this, for it is a matter of course that only definite and concrete ideas (those that have assumed a living form, as it were) can be incorporated by an art.[1] But no instrumental composition can describe the ideas of love, wrath, or fear, since there is no causal nexus between these ideas and certain combinations of sound. Which of the elements inherent in these ideas, then, does music turn to account so effectually? Only the element of motion —in the wider sense, of course, according to which the increas-

---

[1] Vischer (*Aesth.*, § 2, note) defines determinate ideas as the domains of life, provided that the corresponding realities be assumed to agree with our conceptions. For conception always denotes the pure and faultless image of the reality.

ing and decreasing force of a single note or chord is "motion" also. This is the element which music has in common with our emotions and which, with creative power, it contrives to exhibit in an endless variety of forms and contrasts.

Though the idea of motion appears to us a most far-reaching and important one, it has hitherto been conspicuously disregarded in all inquiries into the nature and action of music.

Whatever else there is in music that apparently pictures states of feeling is symbolical.

Sounds, like colors, are originally associated in our minds with certain symbolical meanings which produce their effects independently of and antecedently to any design of art. Every color has a character of its own; it is not a mere cipher into which the artist blows the breath of life, but a force. Between it and certain states of mind, Nature herself has established a sympathetic connection. Are we not all acquainted with the unsophisticated meanings of colors, so dear to the popular imagination, which cultured minds have exalted into poetic refinement? Green is associated with a feeling of hope, blue with fidelity. Rosenkranz recognizes "graceful dignity" in orange, "philistine politeness" in violet, etc. (*Psychologie*, 2nd ed., p. 102.)

In like manner, the first elements of music, such as the various keys, chords, and timbres, have severally a character of their own. There exists, in fact, a but-too-ready art of interpreting the meanings of musical elements. Schubart's symbolism of the keys in music forms a counterpart, as it were, to Goethe's interpretation of colors. Such elements (sounds, colors), however, when employed for the purposes of art, are subject to laws quite distinct from those upon which the effect of their isolated action depends. When looking at a historical painting we should never think of construing the red appearing in it as always meaning joy, or the white as always meaning innocence. Just as little in a symphony would the key of A flat major always awaken romantic feelings or the key of B minor always misanthropic ones, every triad a feeling of satisfaction and every diminished seventh a feeling of despair. Aesthetically speaking, such primordially distinctive traits are nonexistent when viewed in the light of those wider laws to which they are subordinate. The relation in question cannot for a moment be assumed to express or represent anything definite whatsoever. We called it "symbolical" because the subject is exhibited not directly but in a form essentially different from it. If yellow is the emblem of jealousy, the key of G major that of gaiety, the cypress that of mourning, such interpretations, and the definite character of our emotions, imply a psychophysiological relation. The color, the sound, or the plant as such are not related to our emotions, but only the meanings we ourselves attach to them. We cannot, therefore, speak of an isolated chord as representing a determinate feeling, and much less can we do so when it occurs in a connected piece of music.

Beyond the analogy of motion, and the symbolism of sounds, music possesses no means for fulfilling its alleged mission.

Seeing, then, how easy it is to deduce from the inherent nature of sound the inability of music to represent definite emotions, it seems almost incredible that our everyday experience should nevertheless have failed firmly to establish this fact. Let those who, when listening to some instrumental composition, imagine the strings to quiver with a profusion of feeling clearly show what feeling is the subject of the music. The experiment is indispensable. If, for instance, we were to listen to Beethoven's "Overture to Prometheus," an attentive and musical ear would successively discover more or less the following: the notes of the first bar, after a fall into the lower fourth, rise gently and in rapid succession, a movement repeated in the second bar. The third and fourth bars continue it in wider limits. The jet propelled by the fountain comes trickling down in drops, but rises once more, only to repeat in the following four bars the figure of the preceding four. The listener thus perceives that the first and second bars of the melody are symmetrical, that these two bars and the succeeding two are likewise so, and that the same is true of the wider arc of the first four bars and the corresponding arc of the following four. The bass which indicates the rhythm marks the beginning of each of the first three bars with one single beat, the fourth with two beats, while the same rotation is observed in the next four bars. The fourth bar, therefore, is different from the first three, and, this point of difference becoming symmetrical through being repeated in the following four bars, agreeably impresses the ear as an unexpected development within the former limits. The harmony of the theme exhibits the same correspondence of one large and two small arcs: the common chord of C of the first four bars corresponds to the chord of $\frac{6}{4}$ of the fifth and sixth, and to the chord of $\frac{6}{5}$ of the seventh and eighth bars. This systematic correspondence of melody, rhythm, and harmony results in a structure composed of parts at once symmetrical and dissimilar, into which further gradations of light and shade are introduced through the timbre peculiar to each instrument and the varying volume of sound:

Any subject other than the one alluded to we absolutely fail to find in the theme, and still less could we state what feeling it represents or necessarily arouses in the listener. An analysis of this kind, it is true, reduces to a skeleton a body glowing with life; it destroys the beauty, but at the same time it destroys all false constructions.

No other theme of instrumental music will fare any better than the one which we have selected at random. A numerous class of music lovers think that it is a characteristic feature only of the older "classical" music to disregard the representation of feelings, and it is readily admitted that no feeling can be shown to form the subject of the forty-eight preludes and fugues of J. S. Bach's *Well-Tempered Clavichord*. However glaringly unscientific and arbitrary such a distinction may be —a distinction, by the way, which has its explanation in the fact that the older music affords still more unmistakable proof that it aims at nothing beyond itself, and that interpretations of the kind mentioned would, in this case, present more obstacles than attractions—this alone is enough to prove that music need not necessarily awaken feelings, or that it must necessarily be the object of music to represent them. The whole domain of florid counterpoint would then have to be ignored. But if large departments of art, which can be defended both on historical and aesthetic grounds, have to be passed over for the sake of a theory,[2] it may be concluded that such a theory is false. Though a single leak will sink a ship, those who are not content with that are at liberty to knock out the whole bottom. Let them play the theme of a symphony by Mozart or Haydn, an adagio by Beethoven, a scherzo by Mendelssohn, one of Schumann's or Chopin's compositions for the piano, anything, in short, from the stock of our standard music; or again, the most popular themes from overtures of Auber, Donizetti, and Flotow. Who would be bold enough to point out a definite feeling as the subject of any of these themes? One will say "love." He may be right. Another thinks it is "longing." Perhaps so. A third feels it to be "religious fervor." Who can contradict him? Now, how can we talk of a definite feeling being represented when nobody really knows what is represented? Probably all will agree about the beauty or beauties of the composition, whereas all will differ regarding its subject. To "represent" something is to exhibit it clearly, to set it before us distinctly. But how can we call that the subject represented by an art which is really its vaguest and most indefinite element, and which must, therefore, forever remain highly debatable ground?

We have intentionally selected examples from instrumental music, for only what is true of the latter is true also of music as such. If we wish to decide the question whether music possesses the character of definiteness, what its nature and properties are, and what its limits and tendencies, no other than instrumental music can be taken into consideration. What instrumental music is unable to achieve lies also beyond the pale of music proper, for it alone is pure and self-sub-

[2] Disciples of Bach, such as Spitta, attempt to remove the difficulty, not indeed by questioning the theory itself, but by ascribing to his fugues and chords an emotional element as eloquent and positive as the most ardent admirer of Beethoven ever detected in the latter's sonatas. This is consistent, at all events!

sistent music. No matter whether we regard vocal music as superior to or more effective than instrumental music—an unscientific proceeding, by the way, which is generally the upshot of one-sided dilettantism—we cannot help admitting that the term "music," in its true meaning, must exclude compositions in which words are set to music. In vocal or operatic music it is impossible to draw so nice a distinction between the effect of the music and that of the words that an exact definition of the share which each has had in the production of the whole becomes practicable. An inquiry into the subject of music must leave out even compositions with inscriptions, or so-called program music. Its union with poetry, though enhancing the power of the music, does not widen its limits.[3]

---

[3] Gervinus in his work *Händel und Shakespeare* (1868) has reopened the controversy respecting the superiority of vocal over instrumental music; but when he calls vocal music "true and genuine music," and instrumental music a product of art which has "lost the spirit of life and has degenerated into a mere outward display," a physical agent for the production of physiological stimuli, he affords the proof, all his ingenuity notwithstanding, that a learned Handel enthusiast may, at the same time, fall into the most singular errors in regard to the true nature of music. Nobody has ever exposed these fallacies more plainly than Ferdinand Hiller, from whose critique on Gervinus' work we select the following notable passages: "The union of word and sound may be of many different kinds. What a variety of combinations lie between the most simple and almost spoken recitative and a chorus of Bach or a finale in one of Mozart's operas! But words and music affect the listener with *equal* force only in the recitative, whether occurring by itself or as a mere exclamation in the midst of a song. Whenever music steps forth in its true character it leaves language, potent language, far behind. The reason (*unfortunately,* one feels almost tempted to say) is not far to seek. Even the most wretched poem, when set to beautiful music, can scarcely lessen the enjoyment to be derived from the latter, whereas the most exquisite poetry fails to compensate for dullness in the musical part. How slender is the interest which the words of an oratorio excite—it is difficult to comprehend how the gifted composer could ever extract from them the material that fascinates our hearts and minds for hours together. Nay, we go still farther, and maintain that the listener as a rule is quite unable to grasp both the words and the music at the same time. The conventional sounds which go to build up a sen-

Vocal music is an undecomposable compound, and it is impossible to gauge the relative importance of each of its constituents. In discussing the effect of poetry, nobody, surely, will cite the opera as an example. Now, it requires a greater effort, but no deeper insight, to follow the same line of thought when the fundamental principles of musical aesthetics are in question.

Vocal music colors, as it were, the poetic drawing.[4] In the

tence in speech must be united in rapid succession, so that our memory may hold them together while they reach the intellect. Music, on the other hand, impresses the listener with the first note and carries him away without giving him the time, nay, the possibility, of reverting to what he has just heard. . . . Whether we listen to the most simple *Volkslied*," Hiller continues, "or are overpowered by Handel's 'Hallelujah' chorus sung by a thousand voices, our delight and enthusiasm are due, in the former case, to the melodious bud that has hardly yet expanded into a flower; in the latter, to the power and grandeur of the combined elements of a whole universe of sound. The fact that one treats of a sweetheart, the other of a world of bliss, in no way helps to produce the primary and instantaneous effect. For this effect is a purely musical one and would be produced even though we did not, or could not, understand the words." (*Aus dem Tonleben unserer Zeit, Neue Folge*, Leipzig, 1871, p. 40, etc.)

[4] This well-known figure of speech is relevant only so long as nothing but the abstract relations between music and words are referred to, quite irrespective of aesthetic requirements, and when the only point to be settled is on which of these two factors the exact and definite meaning of the subject depends. It ceases, however, to be appropriate when the point at issue is, not this abstract relation, but the mode in which the musical material is manipulated. Only in a *logical* (one might almost say "judicial") sense can the words be said to be the essence, and music a mere accessory. The aesthetic demands on the composer are of a far loftier kind and can only be satisfied by purely musical beauty (suited, of course, to the words). When, therefore, we have to establish in the abstract not what music does on being joined to words, but how it ought to set about it in actual experience, we must above all beware of making it the handmaid of poetry and thus making it move within the narrow limits which the drawer sets to the colorist. Ever since Gluck, during the great and salutary reaction against the melodious exaggerations of the Italian school, retreated even beyond the golden mean (just as Richard Wagner has done in our own days), the saying that the words are the "correct and well-sketched drawing" which music has but to color (a remark which occurs

musical elements we were able to discover the most brilliant and delicate hues and an abundance of symbolic meanings. Though by their aid it might be possible to transform a second-rate poem into a passionate effusion of the soul, it is not the music but the words which determine the subject of a vocal composition. Not the coloring but the drawing renders the represented subject intelligible. We appeal to the listener's faculty of abstraction, and beg him to think, in a purely musical sense, of some dramatically effective melody apart from the context. A melody, for instance, which impresses us as highly dramatic and which is intended to represent the feeling of rage can express this state of mind in no other way than by quick and impetuous motion. Words expressing passionate love, though diametrically opposed in meaning, might, therefore, be suitably rendered by the same melody.

At a time when thousands (among whom there were men like Jean Jacques Rousseau) were moved to tears by the air from *Orpheus:*

> *J'ai perdu mon Eurydice,*
> *Rien n'égale mon malheur,*

Boyé, a contemporary of Gluck, observed that precisely the same melody would accord equally well, if not better, with words conveying exactly the reverse, thus:

> *J'ai trouvé mon Eurydice,*
> *Rien n'égale mon bonheur.*

The following is the beginning of the aria in question, which, for the sake of brevity, we give with piano accompaniment but in all other respects exactly as in the original Italian score:

---

in the dedication to *Alceste*) has been repeated *ad nauseam*. If music is to poetry no more than the mere colorist—if in its dual capacity of drawer and colorist it fails to contribute something entirely new which by the inherent power of its beauty sends forth living shoots of its own and reduces the words to a mere framework—then it has reached at best the level of a student's exercise or an amateur's standard of excellence, but not the sublime height of true art.

We, for our part, are not of opinion that in this case the composer is quite free from blame, inasmuch as music most assuredly possesses accents which more truly express a feeling of profound sorrow. If, however, from among innumerable instances we selected the one quoted, we have done so because, in the first place, it affects the composer who is credited with the greatest dramatic accuracy; and, secondly, because several generations have hailed this very melody as most correctly rendering the supreme grief which the words express.

But even far more definite and expressive passages from vocal music, when considered apart from the text, enable us at best to guess the feeling they are intended to convey. They resemble a silhouette, the original of which we recognize only after being told whose likeness it is.

What is true of isolated passages is true also in a wider application. There are many cases where an entirely new text has been employed for a complete musical work. If Meyerbeer's *Huguenots,* after changing the scene of action, the time, the characters, and the plot, were to be performed as "The Ghibellines of Pisa," though so clumsy an adaptation would undoubtedly produce a disagreeable impression, the purely musical part would in no way suffer. And yet the religious feeling and fanaticism which are entirely wanting in "The Ghibellines" are supposed to be the motive power in *The Huguenots.* Luther's hymn must not be cited as counter-evidence, as it is merely a quotation. From a musical point of view it is consistent with any profession of faith whatever. Has the reader ever heard the *allegro fugato* from the overture to *The Magic Flute* changed into a vocal quartet of quarreling Jewish peddlers? Mozart's music, though not altered in the smallest degree, fits the low text appallingly well, and the enjoyment we derive from the gravity of the music in the opera can be no heartier than our laugh at the farcical humor of the parody. We might quote numberless instances of the plastic character of every musical theme and every human emotion. The feeling of religious fervor is rightly considered to be the least liable to musical misconstruction. Yet there are countless village and country churches in Germany in which at Eucharist pieces like Proch's "Alpine Horn" or the finale from the *Sonnambula* (with the coquettish leap to the tenth) are performed on the organ. Foreigners who visit churches in Italy hear, to their amazement, the most popular themes from operas by Rossini, Bellini, Donizetti, and Verdi. Pieces like these and of a still more secular character, provided they do not altogether lose the quality of sobriety, are far from interfering with the devotions of the congregation, who, on the contrary, appear to be greatly edified. If music as such were capable of representing the feeling of piety, a *quid pro quo* of this kind would be as unlikely as the contingency of a preacher reciting from the pulpit a novel by Tieck or an act of Parliament. The greatest masters of sacred music afford abundant examples in proof of our proposition. Handel, in particular, set to work with the greatest nonchalance in this respect. Winterfeld has shown that many of the most celebrated airs from *The Messiah,* including those most of all admired as being especially suggestive of piety, were taken from secular duets (mostly erotic) composed in the years 1711-1712, when Handel set to music certain madrigals by Mauro Ortensio for the Electoral Princess Caroline of Hanover. The music of the second duet,

> *No, di voi non vo' fidarmi,*
> *Cieco amor, crudel beltá;*
> *Troppo siete menzognere*
> *Lusinghiere deitá!*

Handel employed unaltered both in key and melody for the chorus in the first part of *The Messiah,* "For unto us a Child is born." The third part of the same duet, *So per prova i vostri inganni,* contains the same themes which occur in the chorus of the second part of *The Messiah,* "All we like sheep." The music of the madrigal (No. 16, duet for soprano and alto) is essentially the same as the duet from the third part of

The Messiah, "O Death, where is thy sting?" But the words of the madrigal are as follows:

> *Se tu non lasci amore*
> *Mio cor, ti pentirai*
> *Lo so ben io!*

There is a vast number of similar instances, but we need only refer here to the entire series of pastoral pieces from the "Christmas Oratorio" which, as is well known, were naïvely taken from secular cantatas composed for special occasions. And Gluck, whose music, we are taught, attained the sublime height of dramatic accuracy only by every note being scrupulously adapted to each special case, nay, by the melodies being extracted from the very rhythm of the syllables—Gluck has transferred to his *Armida* no fewer than five airs from his earlier Italian operas (compare with the author's *Die moderne Oper,* p. 16). It is obvious, therefore, that vocal music, which in theory can never determine the principles of music proper, is likewise, in practice, powerless to call in question the canons which experience has established for instrumental music.

The proposition which we are endeavoring to disprove has become, as it were, part and parcel of current musical aesthetics, so that all derivative and collateral theories enjoy the same reputation of invulnerability. To the latter belongs the theory that music is able to reproduce visual and auditory impressions of a nonmusical nature. Whenever the question of the representation of objects by musical means (*Tonmalerei*) is under debate we are, with an air of wisdom, assured over and over again that, though music is unable to portray phenomena which are foreign to its province, it nevertheless may picture the feelings which they excite. The very reverse is the case. Music can undertake to imitate objective phenomena only, and never the specific feeling they arouse. The falling of snow, the fluttering of birds, and the rising of the sun can be painted musically only by producing auditory impressions which are dynamically related to those phenomena. In point of strength, pitch, velocity, and rhythm, sounds present to the ear a figure bearing that degree of analogy to certain visual impressions which sensations of various kinds bear to one another. As there is, physiologically speaking, such a thing as a vicarious function (up to a certain point), so may sense impressions, aesthetically speaking, become vicarious also. There is a well-founded analogy between motion in space and motion in time; between the color, texture, and size of an object and the pitch, timbre, and strength of a tone; and it is for this reason quite practicable to paint an object musically. The pretension, however, to describe by musical means the "feeling" which the falling snow, the crowing cock, or a flash of lightning excites in us is simply ludicrous.

Although, as far as we remember, all musical theorists tacitly accept and base their arguments on the postulate that music has the power of representing definite emotions, yet their better judgment has kept them from openly avowing it. The conspicuous absence of definite ideas in music troubled their minds and induced them to lay down the somewhat modified principle that the object of music was to awaken and represent indefinite, not definite, emotions. Rationally understood, this can only mean that music ought to deal with the *motion* accompanying a feeling, regardless of its essential part, with what is felt; in other words, that its function is restricted to the reproduction of what we termed the dynamic element of an emotion, a function which we unhesitatingly conceded to music. But this property does not enable music to represent indefinite feelings, for to "represent" something "indefinite" is a contradiction in terms. Psychical motion, considered as motion apart from the state of mind it involves, can never become the object of an art, because without an answer to the query, What is moving, or what is being moved? an art has nothing tangible to work upon. That which is implied in the proposition—namely, that music is not intended to represent a definite feeling (which is undoubtedly true)— is only a negative aspect of the question. But what is the positive, the creative, factor in a musical composition? An indefinite feeling as such cannot supply a subject; to utilize it an art would, first of all, have to solve the problem: What *form* can be given to it? The function of art consists in *individualizing,* in evolving the definite out of the indefinite, the particular out of the general. The theory respecting "indefinite feelings" would reverse this process. It lands us in even greater difficulties than the theory that music represents something, though it is impossible to define what. This position is but a step removed from the clear recognition that music represents no feelings, either definite or indefinite. Yet where is the musician who would deprive his art of that domain which from time immemorial has been claimed as belonging to it? [5]

This conclusion might give rise to the view that the representation of definite feelings by music, though impracticable, may yet be adopted as an ideal, never wholly realizable, but which it is possible, and even necessary, to approach more and more closely. The many high-sounding phrases respecting the tendency of music to cast off its vagueness and to become concrete speech, no less than the fulsome praises bestowed on compositions aiming—or supposed to be aiming—at this, are proof of the popularity of the theory in question.

Having absolutely denied the possibility of representing emotions by musical means, we must be still more emphatic in refuting the fallacy which considers this the aesthetic touchstone of music.

The beautiful in music would not depend on the accurate representation of feelings even if such a representation were

---

5 What absurdities arise from the fallacy which makes us look in every piece of music for the expression of definite feelings or from the still greater misconception of establishing a causal nexus between certain forms of music and certain feelings, may be gleaned from the works of so keen-witted a man as Matheson. Arguing from his doctrine that our principal aim when composing a "melody should be the expression of an emotion," he says in his *Vollkommener Capellmeister* (p. 230, etc.): "A courante should convey hopefulness." "The saraband has to express no other feeling than awe." "Voluptuousness reigns supreme in the *concerto grosso.*" The *chaconne,* he contends, should express "satiety," the overture "magnanimity."

possible. Let us, for argument's sake, assume the possibility
and examine it from a practical point of view.

It is manifestly out of the question to test this fallacy with
instrumental music, as the latter could be shown to represent
definite feelings only by arguing in a circle. We must, therefore, make the experiment with vocal music as being that
music whose office it is to emphasize clearly defined states of
mind.[6]

Here the words determine the subject to be described;
music may give it life and breath, and impart to it a more or
less distinct individuality. This is done by utilizing as far as
possible the characteristics peculiar to motion and the symbols
associated with sounds. If greater attention is bestowed on
the words than on the production of purely musical beauty, a
high degree of individuality may be secured—nay, the delusion
may even arise that the music alone expresses the emotion
which, though susceptible of intensification, was already im-
mutably contained in the words. Such a tendency is in its
consequences on a par with the alleged practicability of representing a certain feeling as the subject of a given "piece of
music." Suppose there did exist perfect congruity between the
real and the assumed power of music, that it was possible to
represent feelings by musical means, and that these feelings
were the subject of musical compositions. If this assumption
be granted, we should be logically compelled to call those
compositions the best which perform the task in the most
perfect manner. Yet do we not all know compositions of exquisite beauty without any definite subject? We need but
instance Bach's preludes and fugues. On the other hand, there
are vocal compositions which aim at the most accurate ex-

----

[6] In his critiques on vocal music, the author (in common with other
critics who share his opinion), for the sake of brevity and convenience, has
often when speaking of music made use, without any afterthought, of
terms such as "express," "describe," "represent," etc. Now such terms may
without any impropriety be employed so long as we do not lose sight of
their conditional applicability, i.e., of their applicability in a metaphorical
and dynamic sense only.

pression of certain emotions within the limits referred to, and in which the supreme goal is truthfulness in this descriptive process. On close examination we find that the rigor with which music is subordinated to words is generally in an inverse ratio to the independent beauty of the former; otherwise expressed, that rhetorico-dramatical precision and musical perfection go together but halfway, and then proceed in different directions.

The recitative affords a good illustration of this truth, since it is that form of music which best accommodates itself to rhetorical requirements down to the very accent of each individual word, never even attempting to be more than a faithful copy of rapidly changing states of mind. This, therefore, in strict accordance with the theory before us, should be the highest and most perfect music. But in the recitative, music degenerates into a mere shadow and relinquishes its individual sphere of action altogether. Is not this proof that the representing of definite states of mind is contrary to the nature of music, and that in their ultimate bearings they are antagonistic to one another? Let anyone play a long recitative, leaving out the words, and inquire into its musical merit and subject. Any kind of music claiming to be the sole factor in producing a given effect should be able to stand this test.

This is by no means true of the recitative alone: the most elevated and excellent forms of music equally bear out the assertion that the beautiful tends to disappear in proportion as the expression of some specific feeling is aimed at; for the former can expand only if untrammeled by alien factors, whereas the latter relegates music to a subservient place.

We will now ascend from the declamatory principle in the recitative to the dramatic principle in the opera. In Mozart's operas there is perfect congruity between the music and the words. Even the most intricate parts, the finales, are beautiful if judged as a whole, quite apart from the words, although certain portions in the middle might become somewhat obscure without them. To do justice in a like degree both to the musical and the dramatic requirements is rightly considered to be the ideal of the opera. But that for this reason there should be perpetual warfare between the principles of dramatic nicety and musical beauty, entailing never-ending concessions on both sides, has, to my knowledge, never been conclusively demonstrated. The principle involved in the opera is not undermined or weakened by the fact that all the parts are sung—our imagination being easily reconciled to an illusion of this kind—but it is the constraint imposed alike upon music and words that leads to continual acts of trespass or concession, and reduces the opera, as it were, to a constitutional government whose very existence depends upon an incessant struggle between two parties equally entitled to power. It is from this conflict, in which the composer allows now one principle and now the other to prevail, that all the imperfections of the opera arise, and from which, at the same time, all rules important for operatic works are deduced. The principles in which music and the drama are grounded, if pushed to their logical consequences, are mutually destructive; but they point in so similar a direction that they appear almost parallel.

The dance is a similar case in point, of which any ballet is a proof. The more the graceful rhythm of the figures is sacrificed in the attempt to speak by gesture and dumb show, and to convey definite thoughts and emotions, the closer is the approximation to the low rank of mere pantomime. The prominence given to the dramatic principle in the dance proportionately lessens its rhythmical and plastic beauty. The opera can never be quite on a level with recited drama or with purely instrumental music. A good opera composer will, therefore, constantly endeavor to combine and reconcile the two factors instead of automatically emphasizing now one and now the other. When in doubt, however, he will always allow the claim of music to prevail, the chief element in the opera being not dramatic but musical beauty. This is evident from the different attitudes of mind in which we listen to a play or an opera in which the same subject is treated. The neglect of the musical part will always be far more keenly felt.[7]

As regards the history of the art of music, it appears to us that the importance of the celebrated controversy between the disciples of Gluck and those of Piccinni lies in the fact that the question of the internal conflict in the opera caused by the incompatibility of the musical and the dramatic principles was then for the first time thoroughly discussed. The controversy, it is true, was carried on without a clear perception of the immense influence which the outcome would have on the whole mode of thinking. He who does not shrink from the labor—a very profitable labor, by the way—of tracing this musical controversy to its sources [8] will notice in the vast range from adulation down to ill-breeding all the wit and cleverness of French polemics, but likewise so childish a treatment of the abstract side of the question, and such want of deeper knowledge, that the science of musical aesthetics could gain nothing from the endless disputation. The most gifted controversialists —Suard and the Abbé Arnaud on Gluck's side, and Marmontel

---

[7] What Mozart says about the relative positions of music and poetry in the opera is highly characteristic of him. Completely opposed to Gluck, who gave poetry precedence over music, Mozart held that poetry ought to be the obedient child of music. Without a moment's hesitation he proclaims music to reign supreme in the opera, in which it serves the purpose of illustrating the pervading spirit. In support of this, he reminds us that good music will make us forget even the most wretched libretto— whereas a converse instance can scarcely be adduced—and this unquestionably follows from the inherent nature of music. The mere circumstance that it affects our senses more directly and more powerfully than any other art, and engrosses them completely, goes to show that the feelings which the words might arouse must needs retire into the background for a time. The music, moreover, through the organ of hearing (in some apparently unaccountable manner) appeals directly to our imagination and our emotional faculty with a force that temporarily transcends that of the poetry. (O. Jahn, *Mozart*, III, 91.)

[8] The most notable of these polemic writings are to be found in the collection, *Mémoires pour servir à l'histoire de la Révolution opérée dans la musique par M. le Chevalier Gluck* (Naples and Paris, 1781).

and La Harpe of the opposite camp—though repeatedly going beyond the limits of Gluck's critique and into a more minute examination of the dramatic principle of the opera and its relation to music, treated this relation, nevertheless, as one of the many properties of the opera, but by no means as one of the most vital importance. It never struck them that the very life of the opera depended on the nature of this relationship. It is certainly remarkable how very near some of Gluck's opponents, in particular, were at times to the position from which the fallacy of the dramatic principle can be clearly seen and confuted. Thus La Harpe, in the *Journal de Politique et de Littérature* of October 5, 1777, says:

> On objecte qu'il n'est pas naturel de chanter un air de cette nature dans une situation passionée, que c'est un moyen d'arrêter la scène et de nuir à l'effet. Je trouve ces objections absolument illusoires. D'abord, dès qu'on admet le chant, il faut l'admettre le plus beau possible et il n'est pas plus naturel de chanter mal, que de chanter bien. Tous les arts sont fondés sur des conventions, sur des données. Quand je viens à l'opéra, c'est pour entendre la musique. Je n'ignore pas, qu'Alceste ne faisait ses Adieux à Admète en chantant un air; mais comme Alceste est sur le Théatre pour chanter, si je retrouve sa douleur et son amour dans un air bien mélodieux, je jouirai de son chant en m'intéressant à son infortune.

Is it credible that La Harpe should have failed to recognize the security and unassailableness of his position? For, after a while, it occurs to him to object to the duet of Agamemnon and Achilles in *Iphigenia* because "it is inconsistent with the dignity of the two heroes to talk simultaneously." With this remark he quits the vantage ground of the principle of purely musical beauty and tacitly—nay, unconsciously—accepts the theory of his adversaries.

The more scrupulous we are in keeping pure the dramatic element of the opera by withholding from it the vivifying breath of musical beauty, the more quickly it faints away like a bird in the exhausted receiver of an air pump. We have, therefore, no course open but to fall back upon the pure, spoken drama which, at all events, is proof of the impossibility of the opera; unless, though fully aware of the unreality involved, we assign to the musical element the foremost rank. In the true exercise of the art, this fact has, indeed, never been questioned. Even Gluck, the most orthodox dramaturgist, although he originated the fallacy that opera music should be nothing but exalted declamation, did, in practice, often allow his musical genius to get the better of him, and this invariably to the great advantage of the work. The same holds good of Richard Wagner. For the object of these pages, it is enough to denounce emphatically as false Wagner's principal theorem as stated in the first volume of *Oper und Drama:* "The misconception respecting the opera, viewed as a work of art, consists in the fact that the means (the music) is regarded as the end, and the end (the drama) as the means." An opera, however, in which the music is really and truly employed solely as a medium for dramatic expression is a musical monstrosity.[9]

[9] I cannot refrain from quoting some very pertinent remarks by Grillparzer and M. Hauptmann.

Grillparzer calls it "preposterous to make music in the opera the mere handmaid of the text," and he goes on to say: "If music in the opera is only there to say over again what the poet has already expressed, then away with it. . . . He who knows thy power, O melody! which thou, needless of words to explain thy meaning, bringest down from heaven, thither to return, after stirring the depths of our soul—he who knows thy charms will never make thee the humble creature of poetry. To poetry he may, indeed, accord priority (and I think she has a title to it in the sense in which manhood takes precedence of youth), but he will acknowledge the existence of thy own independent realm, and instead of regarding you both in the light of ruler and subject, or even as guardian and ward, he will deem you to be sisters." He holds it to be of supreme importance that no opera be measured by the standard of poetry—for according to that, every dramatico-musical composition is nonsense—but solely by the standard of music.

In another passage Grillparzer says: "The opera composer who is in the habit of putting his music together mechanically will find nothing easier than to adapt his music exactly to the words; whereas he who aims at making his music an organic whole, with inherent laws, will constantly come

One of the inferences to be drawn from Wagner's proposition (respecting the means and the end) is that all composers who have set indifferent librettos to anything better than indifferent music were guilty of a great impropriety, as we ourselves are in admiring such music.

The connection of poetry with music and with the opera is

---

into collision with the words. Every melody or theme has its own laws of construction and development, which to the true musical genius are sacred and inviolable, and which he dare not infringe in deference to the words. The musical prosaist may, indeed, begin and break off anywhere, for fragments and sections can easily be transposed and rearranged; but whoever has a mind for unity and completeness will give the whole or nothing. These remarks must not be construed into a defense of bad librettos; they are merely intended as an excuse and palliation. It is for this reason that Rossini's shallow trifling is superior to Mosel's intellectual parrotry, which destroys the very essence of music in order to stumble along the line already traced by the poet. For this reason again, many incongruities may be shown to exist in Mozart's operas, but none in Gluck's. Lastly, for this reason the much-admired characteristic of music is often but an extremely negative merit, joy being generally expressed by not-sadness, sorrow by not-gladness, gentleness by not-harshness, rage by not-gentleness, love by means of flutes, and despair with trumpets, kettledrums, and double basses. The composer ought to be guided by the *incidents* as they arise, not by the *words*, and if his music is more eloquent he may rightly disregard the libretto." Do not many of these aphorisms, written so many years ago, sound like a condemnation of Wagner's theories and the Valkyrie-style? Grillparzer displays a profound knowledge of the nature of the public when he says: "Those who in the opera look for purely dramatic effects are, as a rule, those who expect musical effects from dramatic poetry—in other words, an effect without a cause." (IX, 144.)

M. Hauptmann, in his letters to O. Jahn, follows a similar line of thought: "It seemed to me [on hearing Gluck's operas] as if the composer was bent, above all, on being true; not musically true but true in respect of the words. This is frequently the highroad to musical failure, for, whereas speech may be abruptly broken off, music ought to slowly die away. Music will ever remain the vowel, in respect to which the word is but the consonant, and here, as always, it is the vowel which plays the principal part, as being the essential and not the auxiliary sound. The music invariably stands out in strong relief, how well soever it may fit the words, and it ought always to be worth listening to for its own sake." (*Briefe an Spohr*, ed. F. Hiller [Leipzig, 1876], p. 106, etc.)

a sort of morganatic union, and the more closely we examine this morganatic union of musical beauty and definite thoughts, the more skeptical do we become as regards its indissolubility.

How is it that in every song slight alterations may be introduced which, without in the least detracting from the accuracy of expression, immediately destroy the beauty of the theme? This would be impossible if the latter were inseparably connected with the former. Again, how is it that many a song, though adequately expressing the drift of the poem, is nevertheless quite intolerable? The theory that music is capable of expressing emotions furnishes us with no explanation. In what, then, consists the beautiful in music, if it does not consist in the emotional element?

An altogether different and independent element remains, which we shall presently examine more closely.

CHAPTER III

THE BEAUTIFUL IN MUSIC

So far we have considered only the negative aspect of the question, and have sought to expose the fallacy that the beautiful in music depends upon the accurate expression of feelings.

We must now, by way of completing the exposition, bring to light also its positive aspect, and endeavor to determine the nature of the beautiful in music.

Its nature is specifically musical. By this we mean that the beautiful is not contingent upon nor in need of any subject introduced from without, but that it consists wholly of sounds artistically combined. The ingenious co-ordination of intrinsically pleasing sounds, their consonance and contrast, their flight and reapproach, their increasing and diminishing strength—this it is which, in free and unimpeded forms, presents itself to our mental vision.

The primordial element of music is euphony, and rhythm is its soul: rhythm in general, or the harmony of a symmetrical structure, and rhythm in particular, or the systematically reciprocal motion of its several parts within a given measure. The crude material which the composer has to fashion, the vast profusion of which it is impossible to estimate fully, is the entire scale of musical notes and their inherent adaptability to an endless variety of melodies, harmonies, and rhythms. Melody, unexhausted, nay, inexhaustible, is preeminently the source of musical beauty. Harmony, with its countless modes of transforming, inverting, and intensifying, offers the material for constantly new developments; while rhythm, the main artery of the musical organism, is the regulator of both, and enhances the charms of the timbre in its rich variety.

47

To the question: What is to be expressed with all this material? the answer will be: Musical ideas. Now, a musical idea reproduced in its entirety is not only an object of intrinsic beauty but also an end in itself, and not a means for representing feelings and thoughts.

The essence of music is sound and motion.

The arabesque, a branch of the art of ornamentation, dimly betokens in what manner music may exhibit forms of beauty though no definite emotion be involved. We see a plexus of flourishes, now bending into graceful curves, now rising in bold sweeps; moving now toward, and now away from each other; correspondingly matched in small and large arcs; apparently incommensurable, yet duly proportioned throughout; with a duplicate or counterpart to every segment; in fine, a compound of oddments, and yet a perfect whole. Imagine now an arabesque, not still and motionless, but rising before our eyes in constantly changing forms. Behold the broad and delicate lines, how they pursue one another; how from a gentle curve they rise up into lofty heights, presently to descend again; how they widen and contract, surprising the eye with a marvelous alternation of quiescence and mobility. The image thus becomes nobler and more exalted. If, moreover, we conceive this living arabesque as the active emanation of inventive genius, the artistic fullness of whose imagination is incessantly flowing into the heart of these moving forms, the effect, we think, will be not unlike that of music.

When young, we have probably all been delighted with the ever-changing tints and forms of a kaleidoscope. Now, music is a kind of kaleidoscope, though its forms can be appreciated only by an infinitely higher ideation. It brings forth a profusion of beautiful tints and forms, now sharply contrasted and now almost imperceptibly graduated; all logically connected with each other, yet all novel in their effect; forming, as it were, a complete and self-subsistent whole, free from any alien admixture. The main difference consists in the fact that the musical kaleidoscope is the direct product of a creative mind, whereas the optic one is but a cleverly constructed mechanical toy. If, however, we stepped beyond the bounds of analogy, and in real earnest attempted to raise mere color to the rank of music by foisting on one art the means of another, we should be landed in the region of such puerile contrivances as the "color piano" or the "ocular organ," though these contrivances significantly prove both phenomena to have, morphologically, a common root.

If any sentimental lover of music thinks that analogies such as the one mentioned are degrading to the art, we reply that the only question is whether they are relevant or not. A subject is not degraded by being studied. If we wish to disregard the attributes of motion and successive formation, which render a comparison with the kaleidoscope particularly applicable, we may, forsooth, find a more dignified parallel for beautiful music in architecture, the human body, or a landscape, because these all possess original beauty of outline and color quite irrespective of the intellectual substratum, the soul.

The reason why people have failed to discover the beauties in which pure music abounds is, in great measure, to be found in the underrating by the older systems of aesthetics of the sensuous element and in its subordination to morality and feeling—in Hegel, to the "idea." Every art sets out from the sensuous and operates within its limits. The theory relating to the expression of feelings ignores this fact and, disdainfully pushing aside the act of hearing, it passes on immediately to the feelings. Music, say they, is food for the soul, and the organ of hearing is beneath their notice.

True, it is not for the organ of hearing as such, for the "labyrinth" or the "tympanum," that a Beethoven composes. But our imagination, which is so constituted as to be affected by auditory impressions (and in relation to which the term "organ" means something very different from a channel directed toward the world of physical phenomena), delights in the sounding forms and musical structures and, conscious of their sensuous nature, lives in the immediate and free contemplation of the beautiful.

It is extremely difficult to define this self-subsistent and specifically musical beauty. As music has no prototype in nature, and expresses no definite conceptions, we are compelled to speak of it either in dry, technical terms, or in the language of poetic fiction. Its kingdom is, indeed, "not of this world." All the fantastic descriptions, characterizations, and periphrases are either metaphorical or false. What in any other art is still descriptive is in music already figurative. Of music it is impossible to form any but a musical conception, and it can be comprehended and enjoyed only in and for itself.

The "specifically musical" must not, however, be understood only in the sense of acoustic beauty or symmetry of parts—both of which elements it embraces as of secondary importance—and still less can we speak of "a display of sounds to tickle the ear," or use similar phraseology which is generally intended to emphasize the absence of an intellectual principle. But, by laying stress on musical beauty, we do not exclude the intellectual principle; on the contrary, we imply it as essential, for we would not apply the term "beautiful" to anything wanting in intellectual beauty; and in tracing the essential nature of beauty to a morphological source, we wish it to be understood that the intellectual element is most intimately connected with these sonorific forms. The term "form" in musical language is peculiarly significant. The forms created by sound are not empty; not the envelope enclosing a vacuum, but a well, replete with the living creation of inventive genius. Music, then, as compared with the arabesque, is a picture, yet a picture the subject of which we cannot define in words, or include in any one category of thought. In music there is both meaning and logical sequence, but in a musical sense; it is a language we speak and understand, but which we are unable to translate. It is a highly suggestive fact that, in speaking of musical compositions, we likewise employ the term "thought," and a critical mind easily distinguishes real thoughts from hollow phrases, precisely as in speech. The Germans significantly use the term *Satz* ("sentence") for the logical consummation of a part of a composition, for we know exactly when it is finished, just as in the case of a written or spoken sentence, though each has a logic of its own.

The logic in music, which produces in us a feeling of satisfaction, rests on certain elementary laws of nature which govern both the human organism and the phenomena of sound. It is, above all, the primordial law of "harmonic progression" which, like the curve lines in painting and sculpture, contains the germ of development in its main forms, and the (unfortunately almost unexplained) cause of the link which connects the various musical phenomena.

All musical elements are in some occult manner connected with each other by certain natural affinities, and since rhythm, melody, and harmony are under their invisible sway, the music created by man must conform to them—any combinations conflicting with them bearing the impress of caprice and ugliness. Though not demonstrable with scientific precision, these affinities are instinctively felt by every experienced ear, and the organic completeness and logic, or the absurdity and unnaturalness of a group of sounds, are intuitively known without the intervention of a definite conception as the standard of measure, the *tertium comparationis*.[1]

From this negative rationalness, inherent in music and founded on laws of nature, springs the possibility of its becoming invested also with positive forms of beauty.

The act of composing is a mental working on material capa-

---

[1] "Poetry may utilize the ugly (the unbeautiful) even in a fairly liberal measure, for, as it affects the feelings only through the medium of the ideas which it directly suggests, the knowledge that it is a means adapted to an end will, from the outset, soften its impression, even to the extent of creating a most profound sensation by force of contrast and by stimulating the imagination. The effect of music, however, is perceived and assimilated directly by the senses, and the verdict of the intellect comes too late to correct the disturbing factor of ugliness. It is for this reason that Shakespeare was justified in making use of the horrible, while Mozart was obliged to remain within the limits of the beautiful." (Grillparzer, IX, 142.)

ble of receiving the forms which the mind intends to give. The musical material in the hands of creative genius is as plastic and pliable as it is profuse. Unlike the architect, who has to mold the coarse and unwieldy rock, the composer reckons with the ulterior effect of past sounds. More ethereal and subtle than the material of any other art, sound adapts itself with great facility to any idea the composer may have in his mind. Now, as the union of sounds (from the interdependence of which the beautiful in music flows) is not effected by mechanically stringing them together but by acts of a free imagination, the intellectual force and idiosyncrasy of the particular mind will give to every composition its individual character. A musical composition, as the creation of a thinking and feeling mind, may, therefore, itself possess intellectuality and pathos in a high degree. Every musical work ought to bear this stamp of intellectuality, but the music itself must furnish evidence of its existence. Our opinion regarding the seat of the intellectual and emotional elements of a musical composition stands in the same relation to the popular way of thinking as the idea of immanence does to that of transcendence. The object of every art is to clothe in some material form an idea which has originated in the artist's imagination. In music this idea is an acoustic one; it cannot be expressed in words and subsequently translated into sounds. The initial force of a composition is the invention of some definite theme, and not the desire to describe a given emotion by musical means. Thanks to that primitive and mysterious power whose mode of action will forever be hidden from us, a theme, a melody, flashes on the composer's mind. The origin of this first germ cannot be explained, but must simply be accepted as a fact. When once it has taken root in the composer's imagination, it forthwith begins to grow and develop, the principal theme being the center round which the branches group themselves in all conceivable ways, though always unmistakably related to it. The beauty of an independent and simple theme appeals to our aesthetic feeling with that directness which tolerates no explanation except, perhaps, that of its inherent fitness and the harmony of parts, to the exclusion of any alien factor. It pleases for its own sake, like an arabesque, a column, or some spontaneous product of nature—a leaf or a flower.

There is no greater and more frequent error than to distinguish between "beautiful music" with and without a definite subject. The error is due to the extremely narrow conception of the beautiful in music, leading people to regard the artistically constructed form and the soul infused into it as two independent and unrelated existences. All compositions are accordingly divided into full and empty "champagne bottles"; musical "champagne," however, has the peculiarity of developing with the bottle.

One musical thought is refined in and through itself and, for no further reason, another is vulgar; this final cadence is imposing, while by the alteration of but two notes it becomes commonplace. We are perfectly justified in calling a musical theme "grand, graceful, warm, hollow, vulgar"; but all these terms are exclusively suggestive of the musical character of the particular passage. To define the musical complexion of a given theme, we often speak in terms used to describe emotions, such as "proud, gloomy, tender, ardent, longing." But we may with equal justice select them from a different order of phenomena, and call a piece of music "sweet, fresh, cloudy, cold." To be descriptive of the character of a musical composition, our feelings must be regarded in the light of mere phenomena, just like any other phenomenon which happens to present certain analogies. Epithets such as we have mentioned may be used so long as we remain fully conscious of their figurative sense—nay, we may even be unable to avoid them; but let us never say, This piece of music "expresses" pride, etc.

A close examination of the musical definiteness of a theme convinces us, however—the inscrutability of the ultimate ontological causes notwithstanding—that there are various proximate causes with which the intellectual element in a composition is intimately associated. Every musical factor (such as an interval, the timbre, a chord, the rhythm, etc.) has a distinctive feature of its own and its individual mode of action. Though the composer's mind be a mystery, its product is quite within the grasp of our understanding.

A theme harmonized with the common chord sounds different if harmonized with the chord of the sixth; a melody progressing by an interval of the seventh produces an effect quite distinct from one progressing by an interval of the sixth. The rhythm, the volume of sound, or the timbre—each alters the specific character of a theme entirely; in fine, every single musical factor necessarily contributes to a certain passage assuming just *this* particular aspect, and affecting the listener in *this* particular way. What it is that makes Halévy's music appear fantastic, that of Auber graceful—what enables us immediately to recognize Mendelssohn or Spohr—all this may be traced to purely musical causes, without having recourse to the mysterious element of the feelings.

On the other hand, why the frequent chords of $\frac{6}{4}$ and the concise, diatonic themes of Mendelssohn, the chromatic and enharmonic music of Spohr, the short two-bar rhythm of Auber, etc., invariably produce this specific impression and none other—this enigma, it is true, neither psychology nor physiology can solve.

If, however, we inquire into the proximate cause—and that is, after all, what concerns us most in any art—we shall find that the thrilling effect of a theme is owing, not to the supposed extreme grief of the composer, but to the extreme intervals; not to the beating of his heart, but to the beating of the drums; not to the craving of his soul, but to the chromatic progression of the music. The link connecting the two we would by no means ignore; on the contrary, we shall presently subject it to a careful analysis. Meanwhile, we must remember that a scientific inquiry into the effect of a theme can deal only with such musical factors as have an enduring and objective existence, and not with the presumable state of mind in which the composer happened to be. The conclusion reached by arguing from the composer's state of mind directly to the effect of the music might, perchance, be correct; but the most important part of the syllogism, the middle term, i.e., the music itself, would thus be ignored.

A good composer, perhaps more by intuition than by rote, always has a *practical* knowledge of the character of every musical element; but in order to give a rationale of the various musical sensations and impressions we require a *theoretical* knowledge of those characters from the most intricate combinations down to scarcely distinguishable gradations. The specific effect of a melody must not be taken as "a marvel mysterious and unaccountable" which we can only "feel" or "divine"; but it is the inevitable result of the musical factors united in this particular manner. A short or long rhythm, a diatonic or chromatic progression—each has its individual physiognomy and an effect of its own. An intelligent musician will, therefore, get a much clearer notion of the character of a composition which he has not heard himself by being told that it contains, for instance, too many diminished sevenths, or too many tremolos, than by the most poetic description of the emotional crises through which the listener passed.

To ascertain the nature of each musical factor, its connection with a specific effect—its proximate, not its ultimate cause—and, finally, to explain these particular observations by more general laws, would be to establish that "philosophic foundation of music" to which so many writers aspire, though none has ever told us in what sense he understands this phrase. The psychical or physical effect of a chord, a rhythm, or an interval is not accounted for by saying that this is the expression of hope, that the expression of disappointment—as we should say this is red, that green—but only by placing specifically musical attributes in general aesthetic categories, and the latter under one supreme principle. After having explained the isolated action of each single element, it would be incumbent upon us to show in what manner they govern and modify one another in all their various combinations. Most music critics have ascribed the intellectual merit of a composition more particularly to the harmony and the contrapuntal accompaniment. The arguments, however, are both superficial and desultory. Melody, the alleged vehicle of sensuousness and emotion, was attributed to the inspiration of genius—the Italian school accordingly receiving a gracious word of praise; while harmony, the supposed vehicle of sterling thought in contradistinction to melody, was deemed to be simply the result of study and reflection. It is strange how long people were satisfied with so unscientific a view of the subject. Both propositions contain a grain of truth, but they are neither universally applicable nor are the two factors in question in reality ever so strictly isolated. The soul and the talent for musical construction are bound up in one inseparable whole. Melody and harmony issue simultaneously in one and the same armor from the composer's mind. Neither the principle of subordination nor that of contrast affects the nature of the relation of harmony to melody. Both may display now an equal force of independent development, and now an equally strong tendency to voluntary subordination—yet, in either case, supreme intellectual beauty may be attained. Is it, perchance, the (altogether absent) harmony in the principal themes of Beethoven's overture to *Coriolanus* or of Mendelssohn's overture to *The Hebrides* which gives them the character of profound thought? Is the intellectual merit of Rossini's theme "Oh, Matilda!" or of some Neapolitan song likely to be enhanced by substituting for the original meager harmony a *basso continuo* or some complicated succession of chords? The theme was conceived with *that* harmony, *that* rhythm, and *that* instrumentation. The intellectual merit lies in the union of all these factors; hence the mutilation of one entails that of the others. The prominence of the melody, the rhythm, or the harmony, as the case may be, improves the effect of the whole, and it is sheer pedantry to say that the excellence or the triviality is owing here to the presence of certain chords, and there to their absence. The camellia is destitute of odor, and the lily of color; the rose is rich both in odor and color; each is beautiful, and yet their respective attributes cannot be interchanged.

A "philosophic foundation of music" would first of all require us, then, to determine the definite conceptions which are invariably connected with each musical element and the nature of this connection. The double requirement of a strictly scientific framework and an extremely comprehensive casuistry renders it a most arduous though not an impossible task, unless, indeed, our ideal is that of a science of music in the sense in which chemistry and physiology are sciences!

The manner in which the creative act takes place in the mind of a composer of instrumental music gives us a very clear insight into the peculiar nature of musical beauty. A musical idea originates in the composer's imagination; he develops it—more and more crystals coalesce with it, until by imperceptible degrees the whole structure in its main features appears before him. Nothing then remains to be done but to examine the composition, to regulate its rhythm and modify it according to the canons of the art. The composer of instrumental music never thinks of representing a definite subject; otherwise he would be placed in a false position, rather outside than within the domain of music. His composition in such a case would be program music, unintelligible without the program. If this brings the name of Berlioz to mind, we do not thereby call into question or underrate his brilliant talent. In his steps followed Liszt, with his much weaker "Symphonic Poems."

As the same block of marble may be converted by one sculptor into the most exquisite forms, by another into a clumsy botch, so the musical scale, by different manipulation, becomes now an overture of Beethoven, and now one of Verdi. In what respect do they differ? Is it that one of them expresses more exalted feelings, or the same feelings more accurately? No, but simply because its musical structure is more beautiful. One piece of music is good, another bad, because one composer invents a theme full of life, another a commonplace one; because the former elaborates his music with ingenious originality, whereas with the latter it becomes, if anything, worse and worse; because the harmony in one case is varied and novel, whereas in the other it drags on miserably in its poverty; because in one the rhythm is like a pulse, full of strength and vitality, whereas in the other it is not unlike a tattoo.

There is no art which, like music, uses up so quickly such a variety of forms. Modulations, cadences, intervals, and harmonious progressions become so hackneyed within fifty, nay, thirty years, that a truly original composer cannot well employ them any longer, and is thus compelled to think of a new musical phraseology. Of a great number of compositions which rose far above the trivialities of their day, it would be quite correct to say that there *was* a time when they were beautiful. Among the occult and primitive affinities of the musical elements and the myriads of possible combinations, a great composer will discover the most subtle and unapparent ones. He will call into being forms of music which seemingly are conceived at the composer's pure caprice and yet, for some mysterious and unaccountable reason, stand to each other in the relation of cause and effect. Such compositions in their entirety, or fragments of them, may without hesitation be said to contain the "spark of genius." This shows how mistaken Oulibicheff is when he asserts that instrumental music cannot possibly be *spirituel* because the *esprit* of the composer consists solely in adapting his music in "a certain manner to a direct or indirect program." In our opinion we are quite warranted in saying that the celebrated D sharp in the allegro or the descending *unisono* passage in the overture to *Don Giovanni* are imbued with the spirit of genius. The former, however, as little represents (as Oulibicheff imagines) "Don Giovanni's hostile attitude to the human race" as the latter does "the parents, the husbands, the brothers, and the lovers of the women whom Don Giovanni seduced." Such interpretations are not only questionable in themselves, but are particularly so in respect to Mozart, who—the greatest musical genius the world has ever seen—transformed into music all he touched. Oulibicheff also thinks that Mozart's G minor symphony accurately describes the history of a passionate amour in four different phases. But the G minor symphony is music, neither more nor less; and that is quite enough. If, instead of looking for the expression of definite states of mind or certain events in musical works, we seek music only, we shall then, free from other associations, enjoy the perfections it so abundantly affords. Wherever musical beauty is wanting, no meaning, however profound, which sophistical subtlety may read into the work can ever compensate for it; and where it exists, the meaning is a matter of indifference. It directs our musical judgment, at all events, into a wrong channel. The same people who regard music as a mode in which the human intellect finds expression—which it neither is nor ever can be, on account of its inability to impart *convictions*—these very people have also brought the word "intention" into vogue. But in music there is no "intention" that can make up for "invention." Whatever is not clearly contained in the music is to all intents and purposes nonexistent, and what it does contain has passed the stage of mere intention. The saying, "He intends something," is generally used in a eulogistic sense. To us it seems rather to imply an unfavorable criticism which, translated into plain language, would run thus: The composer would like to produce something, but he cannot. Now, an *art* is *to do* something, and he who cannot do anything takes refuge in "intentions."

As the musical elements of a composition are the source of its beauty, so are they likewise the source of the laws of its construction. A great number of false and confused notions are entertained on this subject, but we will single out only one. We mean the commonly accepted theory of the sonata and the symphony, grounded on the assumption that feelings are expressible by musical means. In accordance with this theory, the task of the composer is to represent in the several parts of the sonata four states of mind, all differing among themselves, and yet related to one another. (How?) In order to account for the connection which undoubtedly exists between the various parts, and to explain the differences in their effect, it is naïvely taken for granted that a definite feeling underlies each of them. The construction put upon them sometimes fits, but more frequently it does not, and it never follows as a necessary consequence. It will always, however, be a matter of course that the four different parts are bound up in a harmonious whole, and that each should set off and heighten the effect of the others according to the aesthetic laws of music. We are indebted to the inventive genius of M. v. Schwindt for a very interesting illustration of Beethoven's "Fantasia for the Pianoforte" (Op. 80), the several parts of which the artist interprets as representing connected incidents in the lives of the principal actors, and then gives a pictorial description of them. Now, just as the painter transforms the sounds into scenes and shapes, so does the listener transform them into feelings and occurrences. Both stand in a certain relation to the music, but neither of them in a *necessary* one, and it is only with necessary relations that science is concerned.

It is often alleged that Beethoven, when making the rough sketch of a composition, had before him certain incidents or states of mind. Whenever Beethoven (or any other composer) adopted this method, he did so to smooth his task, to render the achievement of musical unity easier by keeping in view the connecting links of certain objective phenomena. If Berlioz, Liszt, and others fancied that a poem, a title, or an event yielded them something more than that, they were laboring under a delusion. It is the frame of mind bent on musical unity which gives to the four parts of a sonata the character of an organically related whole, and not their connection with an object which the composer may have in view. Where the latter denied himself the luxury of these poetic leading strings and followed purely musical inspiration, we shall find no other than a musical unity of parts. Aesthetically speaking, it is utterly indifferent whether Beethoven really did associate all his works with certain ideas. We do not know them, and as far as the composition is concerned, they do not exist. It is the composition itself, apart from all comment, which has to be judged; and as the lawyer completely ignores whatever is not in his brief, so aesthetic criticism must disregard whatever lies outside the work of art. If the several parts of a composition bear the stamp of unity, their correlation must have its root in musical principles.[2]

To avoid even the possibility of misapprehension, we will now define our conception of the "beautiful in music" from three points of view. The "beautiful in music," in the

[2] Beethoven oracles like Mr. Lobe and others were greatly scandalized at these remarks. By way of replying, we cannot do better than quote Otto Jahn's views in his essay on the new edition of Beethoven's works published by Breitkopf and Härtel (*Gesammelte Aufsätze über Musik*), which fully confirm our own opinions. Citing Schindler's well-known anecdote that, when asked as to the meaning of his D minor and F minor sonatas, Beethoven replied, "Read Shakespeare's *Tempest*," Jahn goes on to say that the querist, after having read the play, will doubtless become convinced that Shakespeare's *Tempest* did not affect him in the same manner as it did Beethoven, and that it failed to inspire him with D minor and F minor sonatas. That just this play should have suggested to Beethoven those musical marvels is certainly an interesting fact; but the attempt to understand them by the light of Shakespeare would be proof of a somewhat beclouded musical judgment. When composing the adagio of his F major quartet (Op. 18, No. 1), Beethoven is said to have had the tomb scene in *Romeo and Juliet* in his mind. Now, if one were to read the scene carefully and keep it in his mind's eye while listening to the music, would this enhance or spoil the enjoyment of the composition? Titles and footnotes, even authentic ones by Beethoven himself, are not calculated to lead to a clearer apprehension of the spirit and drift of the work. On the contrary, such factors are apt to give rise to fallacies and misconceptions, as some of Beethoven's titles have actually done. It is a well-known fact that the charming sonata in E flat major (Op. 81) bears the following inscription, *Les adieux, l'absence, le retour,* and being thought a reliable instance of program music, it is interpreted with every confidence. "That they are incidents in the life of a loving couple," says Marx, who leaves it, however, an open question whether the lovers are married or not, "was, of course, to be presumed; but the music itself contains the proof of it." "The lovers spread out their arms as migratory birds do their wings," says Lenz, with reference to the concluding passages of the sonata. Now it so happens that Beethoven wrote on the original of the first part, "The farewell on the occasion of his Imperial Highness, the Archduke Rudolf's departure, the 4th of May, 1809," and on the title page of the second part, "The arrival of his Imperial Highness the Archduke Rudolf, the 30th of January, 1810." How he would have ridiculed the imputation that he desired to impersonate toward the Archduke "the female flapping her wings and dying with bliss and fond caresses." "It is, therefore, a matter for con-

specific sense in which we understand it, is neither confined to the "classical style" nor does it imply a preference for this over the "romantic style." It may exist in one style no less than the other, and may occur in Bach as well as in Beethoven, in Mozart as well as in Schumann. Our proposition is thus above all suspicion of partisanship. The whole course of the present inquiry never approaches the question of what *ought to be*, but simply of what *is*. We can deduce from it no definite ideal of the truly beautiful in music, but it enables us to show what is equally beautiful even in the most opposite styles.

Not long since, the fashion began to regard works of art in connection with the ideas and events of the time which gave them birth. This connection is undeniable and probably exists also in music. Being a product of the human mind, it must naturally bear some relation to the other products of mind: to contemporaneous works of poetry and the fine arts; to the state of society, literature, and the sciences of the period; and, finally, to the individual experiences and convictions of the author. To observe and demonstrate the existence of this connection in the case of certain composers and works is not only a justifiable proceeding but also a true gain to knowledge. We should, nevertheless, always remember that parallelisms between specific works of art and the events of certain epochs belong to the history of art rather than to the science of aesthetics. Though methodological considerations may render it necessary to connect the history of art with the science of aesthetics, it is yet of the utmost importance that the proper domain of each of these sciences be rigorously guarded from encroachment by the other. The historian viewing a work of art in all its bearings may discover in Spontini "the expression of French imperialism," in Rossini "the political restoration"; but the student of aesthetics must restrict himself to the examination of the works themselves, in order to determine what

---

gratulation," Jahn remarks in conclusion, "that Beethoven (as a rule) refrained from uttering words calculated to beguile people into the belief that he who understands the title, understands also the composition. His *music* says all he wished to say."

is beautiful in them and why it is so. The aesthetic inquirer
knows nothing (nor can he be expected to know anything)
about the personal circumstances or the political surroundings
of the composer—he hears and believes nothing but what the
music itself contains. He will, therefore, without knowing the
name or the biography of the author, detect in Beethoven's
symphonies impetuousness and struggle, unsatisfied longing
and defiance, all supported by a consciousness of strength. But
he could never glean from his works that the composer fa-
vored republicanism, that he was a bachelor and deaf, or any
of the numerous circumstances on which the art historian is
wont to dilate; nor could such facts enhance the merit of the
music. It may be very interesting and praiseworthy to compare
the various schools of philosophy to which Bach, Mozart, and
Haydn belonged, and to draw a parallel between them and
the works of these composers. It is, however, a most arduous
undertaking, and one which can but open the door to fallacies in proportion as it attempts to establish causal relations.
The danger of exaggeration is exceedingly great once this
principle is accepted. The slender influence of contemporari-
ness may easily be construed as an inherent necessity, and the
ever-untranslatable language of music be interpreted in the
way which best fits the particular theory: all depends on the
reasoning abilities; the same paradox which in the mouth of
an accomplished dialectician appears a truism seems the
greatest nonsense in the mouth of an unskilled speaker.

Hegel, too, by his dissertation on music, has been the cause
of misconceptions, for he quite unconsciously confounded the
point of view of art history, which was pre-eminently his own,
with that of pure aesthetics, and attributed an explicitness to
music which, as such, it never possessed. The character of a
piece of music undoubtedly stands in some relation to the
character of its author; but for the student of aesthetics the
relation is nonexistent. The abstract notion of a necessary interdependence of _all_ phenomena whatsoever may in its concrete application be distorted into a caricature of the reality.
It requires, nowadays, great moral courage to resist a doctrine

which is advocated with such skill and eloquence, and to openly affirm that "the grasp of historical relations" is one thing and "aesthetic judgment" another.[3] Objectively speaking, it is beyond doubt, first, that the different styles of expression of distinct works and schools are due to completely different collocations of the musical elements; and, second, that what rightly gives pleasure in a composition, be it a severely classical fugue of Bach or the dreamiest nocturne of Chopin, is the beautiful in a musical sense only.

Even less than with the classical does the beautiful in music coincide with one of its branches, the architectonic. The rigid sublimity of superincumbent harmonies, and the artistic blending of the many different parts (in which no isolated segment is ever free and self-sufficient, because the complete work alone is so) have their imprescriptible justification. Yet those imposing and somber pyramids of sound of the old Italian and Dutch schools, and the finely chased salt cellars and silver candlesticks, so to speak, of venerable Sebastian Bach, are but small provinces within the kingdom of musical beauty.

Many schools of aesthetics think musical enjoyment is fully accounted for by the pleasure derived from mere regularity and symmetry; but these never were the sole attributes of beauty in the abstract, and much less so of beauty in music. The most insipid theme may be symmetrical. "Symmetry" connotes proportion only, and leaves unanswered the question: *What* is it that impresses us as being symmetrical? A systematic distribution of parts, both uninteresting and commonplace, often exists in the most pitiable compositions, but the musical sense wants symmetry combined with originality.[4]

3 If I refer here to Riehl's *Musikalische Charakterköpfe*, I do so in grateful acknowledgment of the intellectual enjoyment to be derived from the book.

4 To illustrate this proposition, I make free in quoting the following passage from my work *Die moderne Oper* (Preface, p. vi):

"The celebrated saying that the 'truly beautiful' (who, by the way, is to be the judge of this attribute?) can never lose its charms, even after the greatest lapse of time, is, as far as music is concerned, little more than an empty, though pompous, phrase. Music proceeds on the lines of nature,

Oerstedt, to crown all, carried this Platonic doctrine so far as to cite the circle (for which he claims positive beauty) as a parallel case. Could he himself never have experienced the horror of a completely round composition?

From caution rather than from necessity we may add that the beautiful in music is totally independent of mathematics. Amateurs (among whom there are also some sentimental authors) have a singularly vague notion of the part played by mathematics in the composition of music. Not content with the fact that the vibrations of sound, the intervals, and the phenomena of consonance and dissonance rest on mathematical principles, they feel convinced that the beautiful in a composition may likewise be reduced to numbers. The study

---

which every autumn allows a world of flowers to molder into dust, whence new blossoms arise. Musical compositions being the work of man, the product of a certain individuality, period, or state of civilization invariably contains the germs of slow or rapid decay. Among the great forms of music, the opera is the most composite and conventional, and, therefore, the most transient form. It may sadden us to reflect that even comparatively new operas of a lofty and brilliant order (Spohr, Spontini) have already begun to disappear from the stage. The fact is, nevertheless, beyond dispute, nor can the process be stayed by invectives against the evil 'spirit of the time'—so characteristic of all ages. Time, forsooth, is a spirit, but a spirit which creates its own body. The theater is the forum for the living aspirations of the public, as distinguished from the quiet study of the reader of musical scores. The stage is the life of the drama; the fight for its possession is the drama's struggle for existence. In this battle an inferior work often triumphs over its superior predecessors, if it breathes the spirit of the time and if its pulse throbs in harmony with *our* feelings and desires. Both the artist and the public have a justifiable longing for something new in music, and those critics whose admiration is restricted to older music and who lack the courage to do homage also to modern compositions undermine the productive power of art. The delightful belief in the imperishableness of music must, of course, be given up. Has not every age proclaimed with the same ungrounded assurance the undying beauty of its best operas? How long is it since Adam Hiller of Leipzig declared that if Hasse's operas should ever fail to charm an audience, a state of universal depravity would ensue? How long is it since Schubart, the musical aesthetic of Hohenasperg, pronounced it wholly inconceivable that the composer Jomelli could ever sink into oblivion? And what are Hasse and Jomelli to us at the present day?"

of harmony and counterpoint is looked upon as a kind of cabala, teaching the "calculus," as it were, of musical composition.

Mathematics, though furnishing an indispensable key to the study of the physical aspect of music, must not be overrated as regards its value in the finished composition. No mathematical calculation ever enters into a composition, be it the best or the worst. Creations of inventive genius are not arithmetical sums. Experiments with the monochord, the figures producible by sonorous vibrations, the mathematical ratios of musical intervals, etc., all lie outside the domain of aesthetics, which begins only where those elementary relations cease to be of importance. Mathematics merely controls the intellectual manipulation of the primary elements of music, and is secretly at work in the most simple relations. The musical thought, however, originates without the aid of mathematics. What Oerstedt means by inquiring whether the lifetime of several "mathematicians would suffice to calculate all the beauties in one symphony by Mozart" [5] we, for our part, are at a loss to understand. What is to be, or can be, calculated? Is it the number of vibrations of each note as compared with the next, or the relative lengths of the divisions and subdivisions of the composition? That which raises a series of musical sounds into the region of music proper and above the range of physical experiment is something free from external constraint, a spiritualized and, therefore, incalculable something. Mathematics has as little and as much to do with musical compositions as such as with the generative processes of the other arts; for mathematics must, after all, guide also the hand of the painter and sculptor; it is the rhythmical principle of verse; it regulates the work of the architect and the figures of the dancer. Though in all accurate knowledge mathematics must have a place, we should never attribute to it a positive and creative power as some musicians, the conservatives in the science of aesthetics, would fain have us do. Mathematics and the excitation of feelings are in a similar position—they have a place

[5] *Geist in der Natur* (Ger. tr. by Kannegiesser), III, 32.

in all arts, but in no art is there so much stress laid upon them
as in music.

Between language and music parallels have also frequently
been drawn and attempts made to lay down for the latter
laws governing only the former. The relation between song
and language is patent enough, whether we base it on the
identity of physiological conditions or on the character which
both have in common, namely, that of expressing thoughts
and feelings by means of the human voice. The analogy, indeed, is so obvious as to render further discussion unnecessary.
We admit at once that wherever music is merely the subjective
manifestation of a state of mind, the laws of speech are, in a
measure, also applicable to singing. That under the influence
of passion the pitch of the voice is raised, while the propitiat-
ing orator lowers it; that sentences of great force are spoken
slowly, and unimportant ones quickly—these and kindred facts
the composer of songs, and the musical dramatist especially,
will ever bear in mind. People, however, did not rest satisfied
with these limited analogies; but conceiving music proper to
be a kind of speech (though more indefinite and subtle), they
forthwith deduced its aesthetic laws from the properties of
language. Every attribute and every effect of music was be-
lieved to have its analogy in speech. We ourselves are of opinion that where the question turns on the nature of a specific
art, the points in which it differs from cognate subjects are
more important than the points of resemblance. An aesthetic
inquiry, unswayed by such analogies as, though often tempt-
ing, do not affect the essence of music, must ever advance
toward the point where speech and music irreconcilably part.
Only from beyond this point may we hope to discover truly
useful facts in respect to music. The fundamental difference
consists in this: while sound in speech is but a sign, that is, a
means for the purpose of expressing something which is quite
distinct from its medium, sound in music is the end, that is, the
ultimate and absolute object in view. The intrinsic beauty of
the musical forms in the latter case, and the exclusive domin-
ion of thought over sound as a mere medium of expression in

the former, are so utterly distinct as to render the union of these two elements a logical impossibility.

Speech and music, therefore, have their centers of gravity at different points, around which the characteristics of each are grouped; and while all specific laws of music will center in its independent forms of beauty, all laws of speech will turn upon the correct use of sound as a medium of expressing ideas.

The most baneful and confused notions have sprung from the attempt to define music as a kind of speech, and we may observe their practical consequences every day. Composers of feeble genius, in particular, were only too ready to denounce as false and sensual the ideal of intrinsic musical beauty because it was beyond their reach, and to parade in its place the characteristic significance of music. Quite irrespective of Richard Wagner's operas, we often find in the most trivial instrumental compositions disconnected cadences, recitatives, etc., which interrupt the flow of the melody, and which, while startling the listener, affect to have some deep meaning, though in reality they display only a want of beauty. Modern pieces, in which the principal rhythm is constantly upset in order to bring into prominence certain mysterious appendages and a superabundance of glaring contrasts, are praised for striving to pass the "narrow limits" of music, and to elevate it to the rank of speech. Such praise has always appeared to us somewhat ambiguous. The limits of music are by no means narrow, but they are clearly defined. Music can never be "elevated to the rank of speech"—musically speaking, "lowered" would be a more appropriate term—for music, to be speech at all, would, of course, be a superlative degree of speech.[6]

---

6 We cannot conceal the fact that one of the loftiest productions of genius of all ages has by its grandeur contributed to this favorite fallacy of musical criticism of modern times, which assumes " an inherent propensity in music to become as definite as speech," and "to throw off the yoke of eurythmy." We allude to Beethoven's *Ninth*. This symphony is one of those intellectual watersheds which, visible from afar, and inaccessible, separate the currents of antagonistic beliefs.

Those musicians who value above all things the sublimity of the "intention" and the intellectual importance of an aim distinct from the music,

Our singers always forget this when in moments of intense emotion they ejaculate sentences as though they were speaking and think they thus attain the highest degree of musical expression. It does not strike them that the transition from song to speech is always a descent, so that the highest pitch of

_____

place the *Ninth Symphony* at the head of all music; while the small party who remain faithful to the abjured belief in intrinsic beauty and who contend for purely aesthetic aspirations look upon it with qualified admiration. As may be guessed, it is the finale which is the point at issue, since no difference of opinion is likely to arise among attentive and competent listeners respecting the exquisite, though not faultless, beauty of the first three parts. We ourselves have always regarded the last part as nothing more than the gigantic shadow of a gigantic body. It is quite possible to realize and apprehend the mighty conception of a lonesome and despairing mind, reconciled at last by the thought of universal happiness, and yet to consider the music of the last part wanting in beauty, its genius and individuality notwithstanding. That this view of the symphony is generally received with supreme disfavor we know but too well. In fact, when one of the most profound and accomplished of German scholars attacked the fundamental idea of the composition in the *Augsburger Allgem. Zeitung* in 1853, he at once felt the necessity of humorously describing the article as emanating from a "feeble intellect." He demonstrated the aesthetic monstrosity of an instrumental composition of several parts closing with a chorus, and compared Beethoven to a sculptor who carves the legs, the body, the chest, and the arms of a figure in white marble, but colors the head. One would think that all sensitive listeners must simultaneously experience a feeling of discomfort when the sounds of the human voice suddenly break upon them, because at this point the composition "changes its center of gravity with a jerk and threatens to throw the listener off his balance." Nearly ten years later we had the satisfaction of knowing that the "feeble intellect" was none other than David Friedrich Strauss.

The clever Dr. Becher, on the other hand, who may figure as the representative of a whole class, speaks of the fourth part of the *Ninth Symphony*, in an essay printed in 1843, as a product of Beethoven's "genius which admits of no comparison with any existing composition in point of originality of construction, sublime organization, and boldness of imagination." He assures us that, in his opinion, this work, like Shakespeare's *King Lear* and a dozen other emanations of the human mind in the zenith of poetic inspiration, overtops even its peers—"a very Dawalagiri in the Himalaya of Art." Becher, in common with those who cherish the same views, gives an exhaustive description of the significance of the normal speech sounds deeper than the low notes in singing, though both proceed from the same organ. As mischievous in their practical consequences (if not more so, because of the impossibility of disproving them by actual experiment) are those theories which try to impose on music the laws of development and construction peculiar to speech, as in former days Rameau and Rousseau, and in modern times the disciples of Richard Wagner, have endeavored to do. In this attempt the life of the music is destroyed, the innate beauty of form annihilated in pursuit of the phantom "meaning." One of the most important tasks of the aesthetics of music would, therefore, be that of demonstrating with inexorable logic the fundamental difference between music and language, and of never departing from the principle that, wherever the question is a specifically musical one, all parallelisms with language are wholly irrelevant.

"subject" of each of the four parts and their profound symbolism—but about the *music itself* not a syllable is said. This is highly characteristic of a whole school of musical criticism, which, to the question whether the music is beautiful, replies with a learned dissertation on its profound meaning.

CHAPTER IV

THE EFFECTS OF MUSIC

Though in our opinion the chief and fundamental task of musical aesthetics consists in subordinating the supremacy usurped by the feelings to the legitimate one of beauty—since the organ of pure contemplation from which, and for the sake of which, the truly beautiful flows is not our emotional but our imaginative faculty—yet the positive phenomena of the emotions play too striking and important a part in our musical life to admit of the question being settled simply by effecting this subordination.

However strictly an aesthetic analysis ought to be confined to the work of art itself, we should always remember that the latter constitutes the link between two living factors—the *whence* and the *whither;* in other words, between the composer and the listener, in whose minds the workings of the imagination are never so pure and unalloyed as the finished work itself represents them. Their imagination, on the contrary, is most intimately associated with feelings and sensations. The feelings, therefore, are of importance both before and after the completion of the work, in respect to the composer first and the listener afterward, and this we dare not ignore.

Let us consider the composer. During the act of composing he is in that exalted state of mind without which it seems impossible to raise the beautiful from the deep well of the imagination. That this exalted state of mind will, according to the composer's idiosyncrasy, take the form more or less of the nascent structure, now rising like billows and now subsiding into mere ripples, without ever becoming an emotional whirlpool which might wreck the powers of artistic invention; that calm reflection again is at least as essential as enthusiasm—all these are well-known principles of art. With special reference to the creative action of the composer, we should bear in mind that it always consists in the grouping and fashioning of musical elements. The sovereignty of the emotions, so falsely reputed to be the main factor in music, is nowhere more completely out of place than when it is supposed to govern the musician in the act of composing, and when the latter is regarded as a kind of inspired improvisation. The slowly progressing work of molding a composition—which at the outset floated in mere outlines in the composer's brain—into a structure clearly defined down to every bar, or possibly, without further preliminaries, into the sensitive polymorphous form of orchestral music, requires quiet and subtle thought such as none who have not actually essayed it can comprehend. Not only *fugato* or contrapuntal passages, but the most smoothly flowing rondo and the most melodious air demand what our language so significantly calls an "elaboration" of the minutest details. The function of the composer is a constructive one, within its own sphere analogous to that of the sculptor. Like him, the composer must not allow his hands to be tied by anything alien to his material, since he, too, aims at giving an objective existence to his (musical) ideal and at casting it into a pure form.

Rosenkranz may have overlooked this fact when he notices the paradox (without, however, explaining it) that women, who by nature are highly emotional beings, have achieved nothing as composers.[1] The cause, apart from the general reasons why women are less capable of mental achievements, is the plastic element in musical compositions which, as in sculpture and architecture, though in a different manner, imposes on us the necessity of keeping ourselves free from all subjective feelings. If the composing of music depended upon the intensity and vividness of our feelings, the complete want of female composers as against the numerous women writers and painters would be difficult to account for. It is not the feelings but a specifically musical and technically trained apti-

---

1 Rosenkranz, *Psychologie* (2nd ed.), p. 60.

tude that enables us to compose. We think it rather amusing, therefore, to be gravely told by F. L. Schubart that the "masterly andantes" of the composer Stanitz are the natural outcome of his tender heart;[2] or to be assured by Christian Rolle[3] that a loving and amiable disposition makes it possible for us to convert slow movements into masterpieces.

Nothing great or beautiful has ever been accomplished without warmth of feeling. The emotional faculty is, no doubt, highly developed in the composer, no less in the poet; but with the former it is not the productive factor. A strong and definite pathos may fill his soul and be the consecrating impulse to many a work, but it can never become the subject matter, as is obvious from the very nature of music, which has neither the power nor the vocation to represent definite feelings.

An inward melody, so to speak, and not mere feeling, prompts the true musician to compose.

We have tried to show that the composing of music is constructive in its nature and, as such, is purely objective. The composer creates something intrinsically beautiful, while the inexhaustible intellectual associations of sound enable his subjectivity to reflect itself in the mode of the formative process. Every musical note having its individual complexion, the prominent characteristics of the composer, such as sentimentality, energy, cheerfulness, etc., may, through the preference given by him to certain keys, rhythms, and modulations, be traced in those general phenomena which music is capable of reproducing. But once they become part and parcel of the composition, they interest us only as musical features—as the character of the composition, not of the composer.[4] That which

---

[2] Schubart, *Ideen zu einer Aesthetik der Tonkunst* (1806).

[3] *Neue Wahrnehmungen zur Aufnahme der Musik* (Berlin, 1784), p. 102.

[4] How careful we ought to be when inferring from a composition the character of its composer, and how great the risk is that flights of fancy will take the place of dispassionate research at the expense of truth, has among other instances been shown by the Beethoven biography of A. B. Marx, who based his panegyric on musical predilections, and, scorning a

a sentimental, an ingenious, a graceful, or a sublime composer produces is, above all, *music,* an objective image. Their works will differ from one another by unmistakable characteristics, and each in its complete form will reflect the author's individuality; but all, without exception, were created as independent and purely musical forms of beauty.

It is not the actual feeling of the composer, not a subjective state of mind, that evokes a like feeling in the listener. By conceding to music the power to evoke feelings, we tacitly recognize the cause to be something objective in the music, since it is only the objective element in beauty which can possess the quality of irresistibleness. This objective something is, in this case, the purely musical features of a composition. It is, aesthetically, quite correct to speak of a theme as having a sad or noble accent, but not as expressing the sad or noble feelings of the composer. Even more irrelevant to the character of a composition are the social or political events of the period. The musical expression of the theme necessarily follows from the individual selection of the musical factors. That this selection is due to psychological causes or facts of contemporary history has to be proved by the particular work itself (and not simply by dates or the composer's birthplace), and even when thus established the connection, however interesting it may be, remains a fact belonging solely to history or biography. An aesthetic analysis can take no note of circumstances which lie outside the work itself.

Though it is certain that the individuality of the composer will find a symbolic expression in his works, it would be a gross error from this subjective aspect of the question to deduce conceptions, the true explanation of which is to be found in the objectiveness of the artistic creation. One of these conceptions is style.[5]

---

conscientious investigation of facts, had many of his conclusions categorically refuted by Thayer's exhaustive inquiry.

[5] Forkel is, therefore, quite mistaken in his derivation of the various musical styles from "different modes of thought." According to him, "the style of a composer is due to the romantic, the conceited, the apathetic,

Style in music we should like to be understood in a purely musical sense: as the perfect grasp of the technical side of music, which in the expression of the creative thought assumes an appearance of uniformity. A composer shows his "good style" by avoiding everything trivial, futile, and unsuitable as he carries out a clearly conceived idea, and by bringing every technical detail into artistic agreement with the whole. With Vischer (*Aesthetik,* § 527), we would use the word "style" in music also in an absolute sense and, disregarding the historical and individual meanings of the term, apply the word "style" to a composer as we apply the word "character" to a man.

The architectonic side of beauty in music is brought into bold relief by the question of style. The laws of style being of a more subtle nature than the laws of mere proportion, one single bar, if out of keeping with the rest, though perfect in itself, will vitiate the style. Just as in architecture we might call a certain arabesque out of place, so we should condemn as bad style a cadence or modulation which is opposed to the unity of the fundamental thought. The term unity must, of course, be understood in its wider and loftier acceptation, since it may comprise contrast, episode, and other such departures.

The limits to which a musical composition can bear the impress of the author's own personal temperament are fixed by a pre-eminently objective and plastic process.

The act in which the direct outflow of a feeling into sound may take place is not so much the *invention* of music as its *reproduction*. The fact that from a philosophical point of view a composition is the finished work of art, irrespective of its performance, should not prevent us from paying attention to the division of music into composition and reproduction (one of the most significant classifications of our art) whenever it contributes to the explanation of some phenomenon.

Its value is especially manifest on inquiring into the sub-

the puerile, or the pedantic, carrying bombast, arrogance, coldness, and affectation into the expression of his thoughts." (*Theorie der Musik* [1777], p. 23.)

jective impression which music produces. The player has the privilege of venting directly through his instrument the feeling by which he is swayed at the time, and to breathe into his performance passionate excitement, ardent longing, buoyant strength, and joy. The mere physical impulse which directly communicates the inward tremor as the fingers touch the strings, as the hand draws the bow, or as the vocal chords vibrate in song, enables the executant to pour forth his inmost feelings. His subjectiveness thus makes itself directly heard in the music, and is not merely a silent prompter. The work of the composer is slow and intermittent, whereas that of the player is an unimpeded flight; the former composes for an age, the latter performs for the fruition of the moment. The piece of music is worked out by the composer, but it is the performance which we enjoy. Thus the active and emotional principle in music occurs in the act of reproduction, which draws the electric spark from a mysterious source and directs it toward the heart of the listener. The player can, of course, give only what the composition contains, and little more than a correct rendering of the notes is demanded of him; he has merely to divine and expose the spirit of the composer—true, but it is the spirit of the player which is revealed in this act of reproduction. The same piece wearies or charms us according to the life infused into its performance. It is like one and the same person whom we picture to ourselves, now in a state of rapturous enthusiasm, now in his apathetic everyday looks. Though the most ingenious music box fails to move us, a simple itinerant musician, who puts his whole soul into a song, may do so.

A state of mind manifests itself most directly in music when origination and execution coincide. This occurs in the freest form of extempore playing, and if the player proceeds not so much according to the strict methods of art as with a predominantly subjective tendency (a pathological one, in a wider sense), the expression which he elicits from the keys may assume almost the vividness of speech. Whoever has enjoyed this absolute freedom of speech, in total oblivion of all surroundings, this spontaneous revelation of his inner self, will know without further explanation how love, jealousy, joy, and sorrow rush out of their secret recesses, undisguised and yet secure, celebrating their own triumphs, singing their own lays, fighting their own battles, until their lord and master calls them back, quieted and yet disquieting.

While the player gives vent to his emotions, the expression of that which is played is imparted to the listener. Let us now turn to the latter.

We often see him deeply impressed by a piece, moved with joy or grief, his whole being rising far above purely aesthetic enjoyment, now enraptured, now profoundly depressed. The existence of such effects is undeniable, actual, and genuine, attaining at times supreme degrees, and they are, moreover, so notorious that we need not dwell any further on their description. Here only two questions arise: in what respect the specific character of this excitation of the feelings by music differs from other emotions, and to what extent this operation is aesthetic.

Though all arts, without exception, have the power to act on our feelings, yet the mode in which music displays it is, undoubtedly, peculiar to this art. Music operates on our emotional faculty with greater intensity and rapidity than the product of any other art. A few chords may give rise to a frame of mind which a poem can induce only by a lengthy exposition, or a picture by prolonged contemplation, despite the fact that the arts to which the latter belong boast the advantage over music of having at their service the whole range of ideas on which we know our feelings of joy or sorrow to depend. The action of sound is not only more sudden, but also more powerful and direct. The other arts persuade us, but music takes us by surprise. This, its characteristic sway over our feelings, is most vividly realized when we are in a state of unusual exaltation or depression.

In states of mind where paintings and poetry, statues and architectural beauties fail to rouse us to active interest, music will still have power over us—nay, greater power than at other times. Whoever is obliged to hear or play music while in a state of painful excitement will feel it like vinegar sprinkled on a wound. No other art, under equal conditions, can cut so sharply to the very quick. The form and character of the music lose their distinctiveness; be it a gloomy adagio or a sparkling waltz, we are unable to tear ourselves away from the sounds—we are not conscious of the composition as such, but only of sound, of music, as an undefined and demoniacal power sending a thrill through every nerve of our body.

When Goethe in his old age experienced once again the power of love, a sensibility for music arose such as he had never dreamed of before. Referring to those remarkable days at Marienbad (1823) in a letter to Zelter, he says: "What a stupendous power music now has over me! Milder's voice, Szymanowska's richness of tone—nay, the very performances of the Jägercorps band open my heart as a clenched fist opens to greet a friend. I am firmly convinced that during the first bar I should have to leave your singing academy." Too clear-sighted not to ascribe the effect mainly to nervous excitement, Goethe concludes in the following terms: "You would cure me of a kind of morbid excitability, which is, after all, at the bottom of this phenomenon." [6] From this alone it ought to be clear that the musical excitation of our feelings is often due to other than purely aesthetic factors. A purely aesthetic factor appeals to our nervous system in its normal condition, and does not count on a morbid exaltation or depression of the mind. The fact of its operating with greater intensity on our nerves proves music to have a preponderance of power as compared with other arts. But on closely examining this preponderance, we find it to be qualitative, and its distinctive quality to depend upon physiological conditions. The material element, which in all aesthetic enjoyment is at the root of the intellectual one, is greater in music than in any other art. Music, through its immateriality the most ethereal art, and yet the most sensuous one through its play of forms without any extraneous subject, exhibits in this mysterious fusion of two an-

[6] *Briefwechsel zwischen Goethe und Zelter*, III, 332.

tagonistic principles a strong affinity for the nerves, those equally mysterious links in the invisible telegraphic connection between mind and body.

Psychologists and physiologists alike are fully cognizant of the truth that music acts most powerfully on the nervous system, but neither of them, unfortunately, can offer an adequate explanation. Psychologists will never be able to throw any light on the irresistible force with which certain chords, timbres, and melodies impress the entire human organism, the difficulty being to establish a nexus between certain nerve excitations and certain states of mind. Nor has the marvelously successful science of physiology made any vital discovery toward a solution of this problem.

As regards the musical monographs on this hybrid subject, they nearly all invest music with the imposing halo of a miracle-worker and descant on some brilliant examples rather than institute a scientific inquiry into the true and necessary relation between music and our consciousness. Of such an inquiry alone are we in need and not of the blind faith of a Dr. Albrecht, who prescribes music as a diaphoretic, nor of the incredulity of an Oerstedt, who explains the howling of a dog on hearing music in certain keys by supposing the dog to have been specially trained to it by a system of whipping.[7]

Many lovers of music may not be aware that there is quite a literature on the physiological action of music and its therapeutic application. Rich in interesting curiosities, but alike unreliable in their observations and unscientific in their explanations, most of these musical quacks magnify a highly composite and secondary endowment of music into one of unconditional efficiency.

From the time of Pythagoras (the first, it is said, to effect miraculous cures by means of music) down to the present day, the doctrine has appeared again and again (enriched, however, by fresh examples rather than by new discoveries) that the exciting or soothing effect of music on the human organism may be utilized as a remedy for numerous diseases. Peter Lichten-

---

[7] *Der Geist in der Natur*, III, 9.

thal gives us a detailed account (*Der musikalische Arzt*) of the cure of gout, sciatica, epilepsy, the plague, catalepsy, delirium, convulsions, typhus, and even stupidity (*stupiditas*), merely by the power of music.[8]

These writers may be divided into two classes according to their method of proof.

One class, arguing from the material point of view, seek to establish the curative effect of music by the physical action of the sound waves which, they say, are transmitted by the auditory nerve to the whole nervous system; and the general shock thus resulting induces a salutary reaction in the morbid part of the organism. The feelings arising at the same time are, it is contended, merely the effect of the nervous shock, since not only do emotions produce bodily changes but the latter, in their turn, may produce corresponding emotions.

According to this theory (championed by an Englishman named Webb), which counts among its followers men like Nicolai, Schneider, Lichtenthal, J. J. Engel, Sulzer, and others, music operates on us just as the peals of an organ do on doors and windows, which tremble under the aerial vibrations. In support of this theory cases are mentioned, such as that of Boyle's servant, whose gums commenced to bleed on hearing a saw sharpened, or of people falling into convulsions when the edge of a knife is scraped on glass.

But that is not music, properly so called. The fact that music, in common with those phenomena which so strongly affect our nerves, has sound for its substratum will be found to be one of great importance in respect of certain conclusions to be drawn hereafter; but for our present purpose it is enough to emphasize, in opposition to a materialistic view, the truth that music begins where those isolated auditory impressions terminate; and that the feeling of sadness which an adagio may

8 This doctrine reached the height of confusion with the celebrated doctor, Battista Porta, who, combining the ideas of a medicinal plant and a musical instrument, professed to cure dropsy by means of a flute made from the stalk of the hellebore. A musical instrument made from the wood of the poplar (*Populus*) was to cure sciatica, and one made of cinnamon bark was to cure fainting fits. (*Encyclopédie*, article "Musique.")

awaken and the bodily sensation produced by a shrill or dis-cordant sound are totally different in kind.

The other class of writers (to which belong Kausch and most writers on aesthetics) try to explain the therapeutic effect of music on psychological grounds. Music, they argue, arouses emotions and passions which throw the nervous system into a violent agitation, and a violent agitation of the nervous system produces a healthy reaction in the diseased organism. This train of reasoning, the logical defects of which are too obvious to require specification, is carried so far by these idealistic "psychologists," in defiance of the materialistic school of thought and in utter disregard of the truths of physiology, as to deny (on the authority of an Englishman by the name of Whytt) the connection between the auditory nerve and the other nerves, which, of course, involves the impossibility of bodily transmitting to the entire organism an impression pro-duced on the ear.

The notion of awakening by musical means definite feel-ings such as love, sadness, anger, and delight, which in their turn are to cure the body by salutary excitement, is certainly a plausible one. It always reminds us of the amusing verdict of one of our most distinguished scientists respecting "Goldberg's electromagnetic chains." It was not proved, he said, whether an electric current was capable of curing certain diseases, but it was proved beyond doubt that "Goldberg's chains" were incapable of generating an electric current. Applied to our "musical doctors," this would run thus: It is *possible* that cer-tain emotions may bring about a favorable turn in bodily ail-ments, but it is *impossible* to call forth at will definite emo-tions by musical means.

Both theories—the psychological and the physiological—agree in this, that they infer from questionable premises even more questionable conclusions, and that their practical appli-cation is the most questionable of all. It may be quite admis-sible to justify some method of treatment on logical grounds, but it is rather disagreeable that there is no record of a doctor sending his patient to hear Meyerbeer's *Prophet* in order to cure him of typhus, or of the French horn being used instead of the lancet.

The physical action of music is neither so powerful in itself, nor so certain, nor yet so independent of psychological and aesthetic associations, nor can it be so nicely regulated, as to admit of its being seriously considered a remedy.

Every cure effected by the aid of music must be regarded in the light of an exception, and the success can never be put down to the music alone, being due partly to special causes and often merely to the patient's idiosyncrasy. It is highly significant that the only case in which music is really applied as a remedy is in the treatment of the insane, and this is mainly grounded on the psychological aspect of musical impressions. That in the modern treatment of insanity music is frequently employed with great success is a well-known fact. The success, however, is owing neither to the nervous shock nor to the arousing of the passions, but to the soothing and exhilarating influence which music, at once diverting and fascinating, exerts on a darkened or morbidly excited mind. It is true that the patient listens to the sensuous rather than to the artistic part of the music; yet, if he can but fix his attention, he proves himself capable of aesthetic enjoyment, though in an inferior degree.

Now, in what respect do all these musico-medical works contribute toward a clear knowledge of music? They all confirm what has been observed from time immemorial, namely, that with the "feelings" and "passions" aroused by music there always coexists a strong physical agitation. Once grant the assumption that an integral part of the emotion aroused by music is of physical origin and it follows that the phenomenon, closely related as it is to nerve function, must be studied in this, its physical aspect. No musician, therefore, can expect a scientific solution of this problem without making himself acquainted with the latest results of physiological research into the connection between music and the emotions.

If we follow the course which a melody must take in order to operate on our feelings, we shall find it traced with tolerable accuracy from the vibrating instrument to the auditory nerve, thanks especially to Helmholtz's famous discoveries in this domain of science recorded in his work, *Lehre von den Tonempfindungen.* The science of acoustics has clearly shown what are the outward conditions under which the sensation of sound in general, and of any sound in particular, becomes possible; anatomy, with the help of the microscope, has revealed the most minute and hidden structures of the organ of hearing. Physiology, in fine, though debarred from experimenting directly on the extremely small and delicate constituents of this hidden marvel, has nevertheless to a certain extent ascertained its *modus operandi,* and to a still greater extent explained it by a theory propounded by Helmholtz, so as to render intelligible the whole process by which we become conscious of sound physiologically. Even beyond these limits, in the domain where natural science comes into close contact with aesthetics, much has been elucidated by Helmholtz's theory of consonance and the affinities of sound, which until lately was shrouded in mystery. But this, unfortunately, is the whole extent of our knowledge. The most essential part, the physiological process by which the sensation of sound is converted into a feeling, a state of mind, is unexplained, and will ever remain so. Physiologists know that what our senses perceive as sound is, objectively speaking, molecular motion within the nerve substance, and this is true of the nerve centers no less than of the auditory nerve. They also know that the fibers of the auditory nerve are connected with the other nerves, to which they transmit the impulse received, and that the organ of hearing is connected with the cerebrum and the cerebellum, with the larynx, the lungs, and the heart. About the specific mode, however, in which music affects these nerves they know nothing, nor yet about the different ways in which certain musical factors, such as chords, rhythms, and the sounds of instruments operate on different nerves. Is a sensation of musical sound propagated to all the nerves connected with the auditory nerve, or only to some of them? With what degree of intensity? Which musical elements affect the brain more particularly, and which the nerves supplying the heart and the lungs? It is an undoubted fact that dance music produces in young people (whose natural inclination is not controlled by social restraints) a twitching of the whole body, and especially of the feet. We cannot, without being one-sided, dispute the physiological action of martial or dance music and attribute its effect solely to a psychological association of ideas. Its psychological aspect—the recollection of former pleasures derived from dancing—helps us to understand the phenomenon; but taken alone it does not explain it. The feet do not move because it is dance music, but we call it dance music because it makes the feet move. Whoever glances around in an opera house will notice the ladies involuntarily beating time with their heads to any lively or taking tune, but never to an adagio, however impressive and melodious it may be. Should we infer from this that certain musical factors, and more particularly rhythmical ones, affect the motor and others the sensory nerves? Which affect the former and which the latter? [9] Is the solar plexus, which is reputed to be pre-eminently the seat of sensation, especially affected by music? Or is it the sympathetic ganglia (the best part of which is their name, as Purkinje once remarked to me) which are so affected? Why one sound affects us as shrill and harsh, another as clear and mellifluous, the science of acoustics explains by the irregularity or regularity with which the sonorous pulses follow each other; again, that several simultaneously occurring sounds produce now the effect of consonance and now that of dissonance is ac-

[9] Carus tries to account for the motor stimulus by supposing the auditory nerve to originate in the cerebellum, the latter to be the seat of volition; and the co-operation of the two to be the cause of the phenomenon that auditory impressions incite us to acts of courage, etc. But this is a very lame hypothesis, seeing that science has not yet proved the auditory nerve to originate in the cerebellum. Harless (see R. Wagner's *Manual of Physiology*, "The Function of Hearing") maintains that the mere *perception of rhythmical motion*, apart from auditory impressions, has the same tendency to give motor impulses as rhythmical music. But this doctrine conflicts with our experience.

counted for by the slow or rapid succession of beats.[10] The explanations of more or less simple sensations of sound, however, cannot satisfy the aesthetic inquirer, who demands an explanation of the *feeling* produced, and asks how it is that one series of melodious sounds induces a feeling of sadness, and another, of equally melodious sounds, a feeling of joy? Whence the diametrically opposed moods which often take hold of us with irresistible force on hearing chords and instruments of different kinds, but of equally pure and agreeable sound?

To all this—at least as far as our knowledge and judgment go—physiologists can give no clue! How, indeed, can they be expected to do so? For they can tell us neither why grief makes us weep, nor why joy makes us laugh—nay, they do not even know what grief and joy are! Let us, therefore, never appeal to a science for explanations which it cannot possibly give.[11]

It is true, of course, that the cause of every emotion which music arouses is chiefly to be found in some specific mode of nerve activity induced by an auditory impression. But how the excitation of the auditory nerve (which we cannot even trace to its source) is transformed into a definite sentiment; how a physical impression can pass into a state of mind; how, in fine, a sensation can become an emotion—all this lies beyond the mysterious bridge which no philosopher has ever crossed. It is the one great problem expressed in numberless ways: the con-

[10] Helmholtz, *Lehre von den Tonempfindungen* (2nd ed., 1870), p. 319.

[11] Lotze, one of our most gifted physiologists, says (*Medicinische Psychologie*, p. 237): "A careful study of melodies would extort from us the admission that we know nothing whatever about the conditions under which the change from one kind of nerve excitation to another becomes the physical substratum of the powerful aesthetic feelings which vary with the music." With respect to the feeling of satisfaction or discomfort which a single tone may evoke, he remarks (p. 236): "It is a matter of utter impossibility to offer a physiological explanation for these simple sensations, in particular, as we do not know with any degree of accuracy in what respect the impressing causes affect the nerve function, and we are, therefore, quite unable to determine to what extent they promote or impede it."

nection between mind and body. This sphinx will never throw herself into the sea.[12]

All that the inquiries into the physiological aspect of music have brought to light is of the utmost importance for the correct appreciation of auditory impressions as such, and in that direction considerable progress may yet be made. But with respect to the main issue in music we shall probably never know more than we do now.

The result thus arrived at, when applied to musical aesthetics, leads to the conclusion that those theorists who ground the beautiful in music on the feelings it excites build upon a most uncertain foundation, scientifically speaking, since they are necessarily quite ignorant of the nature of this connection and can therefore, at best, only indulge in speculation and flights of fancy. An interpretation of music based on the feelings cannot be acceptable either to art or science. A critic does not substantiate the merit or subject of a symphony by describing his subjective feelings on hearing it, nor can he enlighten the student by making the feelings the starting point of his argument. This is of great moment; for if the connection between certain feelings and certain modes of musical expression were so well established as some seem inclined to think, and as it ought to be if the importance claimed for it were justified, it would be an easy matter to lead the young composer onward to the most sublime heights of his art. The attempt to do this has actually been made. Mattheson teaches in the third chapter of his *Vollkommener Capellmeister* how pride, humility, and all the other emotions and passions are to be translated into music. Thus he says, "To express jealousy, the music must have something grim, sullen, and doleful about it." Heinchen, another writer of the last century, devotes eight pages in his *Generalbass* to actual examples of the modes in which music should express the "feelings of an impetuous,

12 While revising the fourth edition of this work, the author came across a most invaluable corroboration of the views here set forth in Dubois-Reymond's speech at the Science Congress of 1872 in Leipzig.

factious, pompous, timorous, or lovesick mind." [13] To crown
the absurdity, directions of this kind should commence with
the formula of cookery books: "Take," etc., or with that of
medical prescriptions, "R." Such attempts yield the highly instructive lesson that specific rules of art are always both too
narrow and too wide.

Those inherently fallacious precepts for the excitation of
definite emotions by musical means have so much the less to
do with aesthetics as the effect aimed at is not a purely aesthetic one, an inseparable portion of it being of a distinctly
physical character. An aesthetic prescription would have to
teach the composer how to produce beauty in music, and not
how to excite particular feelings in the audience. How im-
potent these rules are in reality is best proved by considering
what magic power they must possess to be efficacious. For if the
action of every musical factor on our feelings were a necessary and determinable one, we should be able to play on the
mind of the listener as on the keyboard of a piano. And even
assuming this to be possible, would the object of music be attained thereby? This is the only legitimate form of the question, and to it none but a negative reply can be given. Musical
beauty alone is the true power which the composer wields.
With this for his pilot, he safely passes through the rapids of
time, where the factor of emotion would be powerless to save
him from shipwreck.

The two points at issue—namely, what the distinctive trait
is of a feeling aroused by music, and whether this is of an essentially aesthetic nature—are settled by the recognition of one
and the same fact: the intense action on our nervous system.
This fact explains the characteristic force and directness with

[13] Greatly amusing are the discourses of v. Böcklin, Privy Councilor and
Doctor of Philosophy, who in his book *Fragmente zur höheren Musik*
(1811), p. 34, says among other things: "If the composer wants to represent an offended person, outbursts of aesthetic warmth must follow each
other in rapid succession; lofty strains must resound with extreme vivac-
ity; the baritones rave, and terrific blasts inspire the expectant listener
with awe."

which music (as compared with arts that do not employ the medium of sound) is capable of exciting emotions.

But the more overpowering the effect is in a physical, i.e., in a pathological sense, the less is it due to aesthetic causes—a proposition, by the way, the terms of which cannot be inverted. In connection with the production and interpretation of music, another factor must be emphasized, which in antithesis to a specifically musical excitation of the feelings approximates to the general aesthetic conditions of all the other arts. This factor is the act of pure contemplation (*die reine Anschauung*). The next chapter will be devoted to the study of its specific function in music, and of the manifold relations subsisting between it and our sensibility.

CHAPTER V

MUSICAL CONTEMPLATION

The greatest obstacle to a scientific development of musical aesthetics has been the undue prominence given to the action of music on our feelings. The more violent this action is, the louder is it praised as evidence of musical beauty. But we have seen that the most powerful effects of music are mainly to be attributed to physical excitement on the part of the listener. The power which music possesses of profoundly affecting the nervous system cannot be ascribed so much to the artistic forms created by and appealing to the mind as to the material with which music works and which Nature has endowed with certain inscrutable affinities of a physiological order. That which for the unguarded feelings of so many lovers of music forges the fetters which they are so fond of clanking are the primitive elements of music—sound and motion. Far be it from us to loosen the legitimate ties which connect music with the emotions, but the latter, which more or less always coexist with the act of pure contemplation, are of aesthetic value only so long as we remain conscious of their aesthetic origin—that is, so long as the pleasure is solely derived from viewing a thing of beauty, and a thing of beauty in just this particular form.

Where this consciousness is absent; where, while contemplating the work of art, we are laboring under other influences; where the mind is carried away by the purely physical element of sound, art, in the true sense of the word, can pride itself the less on having produced this effect the stronger the effect is. The number of those who thus listen to, or rather feel, music is very considerable. While in a state of passive receptivity, they suffer only what is elemental in music to affect them, and thus pass into a vague "supersensible" excitement

89

of the senses produced by the general drift of the composition. Their attitude toward music is not an observant but a pathological one. They are, as it were, in a state of waking dreaminess and lost in a sounding nullity; their minds are constantly on the rack of suspense and expectancy. If to a musician who considers the supreme aim of music to be the excitation of feelings we present several pieces, say of a gay and sprightly character, they will all impress him alike. His feelings assimilate only what these pieces have in common, but the special features of each composition and the individuality of its artistic interpretation pass unnoticed. The truly musical listener, however, pursues an exactly opposite course. His attention is so greatly absorbed by the particular form and character of the composition, by that which gives it the stamp of individuality among a dozen pieces of similar complexion, that he pays but little heed to the question whether the expression of the same or of different feelings is aimed at. The habit of looking only for some abstract feeling instead of judging the concrete work of art is, in any great measure, practiced in music alone. It may be likened to the peculiar effect of light on a landscape, which strikes some people so forcibly as to prevent them from clearly perceiving the illuminated object itself. A general impression, unreasoned and therefore doubly obtrusive, thrusts itself upon their undiscriminating senses.[1]

Instead of closely following the course of the music, these enthusiasts, reclining in their seats and only half-awake, suffer themselves to be rocked and lulled by the mere flow of sound. The sound, now waxing and now diminishing in strength, now

1 The lovesick duke in Shakespeare's *Twelfth Night* is a poetic personification of this mode of hearing music. He says:

> If music be the food of love, play on,
> Give me excess of it, . . .
> Oh, it came o'er my ear like the sweet south
> That breathes upon a bank of violets
> Stealing and giving odor. . . .

and later on, in the second act, he exclaims:

> Give me some music, . . .
> Methought it did relieve my passion much, . . .

rising up in jubilant strains and now softly dying away, produces in them a series of vague sensations which they in their simplicity fancy to be the result of intellectual action. They are the most easily satisfied part of the audience, and it is also they who tend to lower the dignity of music. For their ear the aesthetic criterion of intelligent gratification is wanting, and a good cigar, some exquisite dainty, or a warm bath yields them the same enjoyment as a symphony, though they may not be aware of the fact. In the indolent and apathetic attitude of some and the hysterical raptures of others, the active principle is the same—delight in the *elemental* property of music. To recent times, by the way, we owe a discovery of the greatest moment for such listeners as merely wish their feelings to be played upon to the exclusion of their intellect—the discovery of a far more potent factor than music. We are alluding to ether and chloroform. There is no doubt that these anesthetics envelop the whole organism in a cloud of delightful and dreamlike sensations, so that there is no longer any need for stooping to the vulgar practice of winebibbing, though it must be confessed that this, too, is not without its musical effect.

From this point of view, musical compositions belong to the class of spontaneous products of nature, the contemplation of which charms us without obliging us to enter into the thoughts of a creative mind, conscious of what it creates. The sweet exhalations of the acacia may be breathed with closed eyes and in a dream, as it were; but creations of the human intellect demand a different attitude of mind, unless we would drag them down to the level of mere physical stimulants.

No other art lends itself so readily to such practices as music, the physical side of which admits the possibility, at least, of an unreasoning enjoyment. The fugitive nature of sound, as compared with the enduring effect of other arts, reminds us most significantly of the act of imbibing.

We may drink in a melody, but not a picture, a church, or a drama. For this reason no other art can be turned to such subservient uses. Even the best music may be performed at a banquet and promote the assimilation of indigestible food. Music is at once the most imperative and the most indulgent of all arts. A barrel organ at our door may force us to *hear* it, but not even a symphony by Mendelssohn can compel us to *listen*.

This objectionable mode of hearing music is by no means identical with the naïve delight which the uncultured masses take in the material aspect of the various arts, while its ideal aspect is manifest only to the trained understanding of the few. The inartistic interpretation of a piece of music is derived, on the contrary, not from the material part properly so called, not from the rich variety of the successions of sounds, but from their vague aggregate effect which impresses them as an undefinable feeling. This explains the unique position which the intellectual element in music occupies in relation to form and substance (subject). The sentiment pervading a piece of music is habitually regarded as the drift, the idea, the spirit of the composition; whereas the artistic and original combination of definite successions of sound is said to be the mere form, the mold, the material garb of those supersensible elements. But it is precisely the "specifically musical" element of the creation of inventive genius which the contemplating mind apprehends and assimilates. These concrete musical images, and not the vague impression of some abstract feeling, constitute the spirit of the composition. The form (the musical structure) is the real substance (subject) of music—in fact, is the music itself, in antithesis to the feeling, its alleged subject, which can be called neither its subject nor its form, but simply the effect produced. In like manner, that which is regarded as purely material, as the transmitting medium, is the product of a thinking mind, whereas that which is presumed to be the subject—the emotional effect—belongs to the physical properties of sound, the greater part of which is governed by physiological laws.

The above considerations enable us to put down at its true value the so-called "moral effect" of music, which is paraded before us as a brilliant counterpart to the already mentioned "physical effect" and which was expatiated on so often by older writers. But music in this sense is not in the remotest degree enjoyed as a thing of beauty, since it acts like a brute force of Nature and may incite us to the most senseless actions. Its function, therefore, is diametrically opposed to truly aesthetic enjoyment, and it is obvious that the alleged moral and the acknowledged physical effects of music have a good deal in common.

The importunate creditor who by his debtor's music is induced to forgive him the whole debt [2] is affected in the same manner as one who by the tune of a waltz is suddenly roused from repose and impelled to dance. The former is moved by the subtle elements of harmony and melody, the latter by the more palpable one of rhythm. Neither acts of his own free will, neither is overwhelmed by a superior mind or by moral beauty, but simply in consequence of a powerful nervous stimulus. Music loosens the feet or the heart just as wine loosens the tongue. But such victories only testify to the weakness of the vanquished. To be the slave of unreasoning, undirected, and purposeless feelings, ignited by a power which is out of all relation to our will and intellect, is not worthy of the human mind. If people allow themselves to be so completely carried away by what is elemental in art as to lose all self-control, this scarcely redounds to the glory of the art, and much less to that of the individual.

It is by no means the object of music to handicap the mind with such tendencies, but its intense action on the emotional faculty renders enjoyment in this sense, at all events, possible. This is the cause of the oldest attacks on music, grounded on the reproach that it enervates, effeminates, and benumbs its votaries.

And this reproach is but too well merited wherever music is performed only to excite "indefinite feelings" and to supply food for the "emotions." Beethoven wanted music "to strike fire in the mind"; at least "it ought to do so," he thought. But

[2] This is related of the Neapolitan singer Palma, and of others. (A. Burgh, *Anecdotes on Music*, 1814.)

is it not just possible that the fire kindled and fed by music may prevent the development of that strength of will and power of intellect which man is capable of?

This stricture on the influence of music seems to us, in any case, more dignified than extravagant praises. As the physical effect of music varies with the morbid excitability of the nervous system, so the moral influence of sound is in proportion to the crudeness of mind and character. The lower the degree of culture, the greater the potency of the agent in question. It is well known that the action of music is most powerful of all in the case of savages.

But that does not discourage these experts in musical ethics. They love to quote as a kind of introduction the numerous instances of "animals even" yielding to the power of music. It is true that the sound of the trumpet inspires the horse with courage and an eagerness for the battle, that the fiddle tempts the bear to waltz, and that both the nimble spider and the clumsy elephant move to its fascinating strains. But is it, after all, so great an honor to be a musical enthusiast in such company?

After these animal accomplishments come the attainments of man. They are mostly of the kind related of Alexander the Great, who became furious on hearing Timotheus perform on the flute, and cooled down under the influence of a song. The less notorious Ericus Bonus, king of Denmark, in order to convince himself of the famous power of music, summoned a renowned musician to play before him, but not until every kind of weapon was put out of reach. By the choice of his modulations, the minstrel first cast on all around him a gloom, which he presently changed into hilarity. This hilarity he gradually worked up into a feeling of frenzy. "Even the king rushed out of the room, seized his sword, and slew four of the bystanders." (Albert Krantzius; dan. lib. v., cap. 3.) And that, be it noted, was "Eric the Good."

If such "moral effects" of music were still in vogue, we should probably be in too chronic a state of indignation ever to have the mental calm necessary for a dispassionate survey of this weird power, which with arrogant "extraterritoriality" subjugates and confuses the human mind without in the least regarding its thoughts and resolutions.

The reflection, however, that the most famous of these musical trophies have been won in the remote past inclines us to view them in the light of history only.

It is beyond all question that the action of music was far more direct in the case of ancient races than it is with us, because mankind is much more easily impressed by elemental forces in a primitive state of culture than later on, when intellectual consciousness and the faculty of reflection have attained a higher degree of maturity. This natural sensitivity was greatly assisted by the peculiar condition of music during the Grecian era. Music of that era was no art in the present acceptation of the term. Sound and rhythm discharged their functions in almost isolated independence, and in their poverty-stricken ostentation took the place of those rich and ingenious forms which constitute the music of our day. All we know about the music of those times points to the conclusion that its function was purely sensuous, though, within such limits, susceptible of considerable refinement. Judged by the modern standard of art, there was no such thing as music in the age of the ancient classics; otherwise it would never have disappeared, but would have played just as important a part in the subsequent development of the art as classical poetry, sculpture, and architecture have done. The love of the Greeks for a profound study of the extremely subtle relations of sound is a purely scientific question and foreign to the present inquiry.

The lack of harmony, the poverty of the melody within the extremely narrow limits of the recitative, and finally the impossibility of expanding the ancient system into a multiformity of truly musical images absolutely disqualified music, as then understood, for the position of an art in a musical sense. Nor had it any really independent function, being always used in connection with poetry, dancing, and pantomimic representation—in other words, as an adjunct of other arts. The sole office of music was to give life to the rhythmical beats, to the sounds of various instruments, and lastly, as an intensification of declamatory recitative, to comment on words and feelings. The action of music was limited, therefore, more particularly to its sensuous and symbolic side. The attention being exclusively directed to these factors, this concentration naturally developed them into effect-producing media of considerable strength—nay, of great subtlety. The music of the present day knows just as little of the prodigious elaboration of the musical material, going to the length of using even "demisemitones" and "the enharmonic family of sound," as of the specific character of each individual key and its close adaptation to the words both spoken and sung. These subtle relations within their narrow sphere, moreover, were destined for the appreciation of a much more sensitive audience. Just as the Greek ear was able to perceive infinitely finer differences of interval than ours—exposed as it is to a constantly varying temperature—so those races were by nature far more susceptible and fonder of emotional changes wrought by music than are we, who take a meditative delight in the ingenious forms which music conjures up, a delight which tends to paralyze the elemental influence of sound. There is no difficulty, therefore, in comprehending why the action of music was more intense in ancient times.

The same applies to a small number of those anecdotes which record the specific effects produced by the several modes of the Greeks. Their explanation is to be found in the scrupulous isolation of the various modes, each mode being selected for a definite purpose to the complete exclusion of any alien admixture. The Doric mode was employed on solemn, and particularly on religious, occasions; by means of the Phrygian the Greeks fired their armies with courage; the Lydian signified mourning and sadness; while wherever the Aeolian resounded love-making and banqueting were the order of the day. This rigid and conventional division into four principal modes answering to as many states of mind, and the circumstance that no poem was ever recited to any but its corresponding mode, could not but give to the mind a decided tendency to recall at the sounds of a certain musical mode the feeling associated with it. As a result of this one-sided culture, music had become an indispensable and docile accessory of all the arts, a means for the attainment of educational, political, and other ends; it was a maid-of-all-work but not a self-subsistent art. If the strains of Phrygian music sufficed to incite warriors to acts of bravery, if the faithfulness of grass widows could be secured by Doric songs, let generals and husbands lament the extinction of the Greek system—students of aesthetics and composers will cast no regrets after it.

This morbid sensitivity, in our opinion, is in direct opposition to the voluntary and pure act of contemplation which alone is the true and artistic method of listening. Compared to it the ecstasies of the musical enthusiast sink to the level of the crude emotion of the savage. The beautiful is not suffered but enjoyed, and the term "aesthetic enjoyment" clearly confirms this fact. Sentimentalists regard it, of course, as heresy against the omnipotence of music to take exception to the emotional revolutions and conflicts which they discover in every musical composition, and of which they never fail to experience the full force. Those who cannot agree with them are "callous," "apathetic," "cold reasoners." No matter. It is, nevertheless, both ennobling and elevating to follow the creative mind as it unlocks with magic keys a new world of elements, and to observe how at its bidding they enter into all conceivable combinations; how it builds up and casts down, creates and destroys, controlling the whole wealth of an art which exalts the ear to an organ of sense of the greatest delicacy and perfection. That which calls forth from us a sympathetic response is not in the least the passion professed to be described. With a willing mind, calm but acutely sensitive, we enjoy the work of art as it passes before us, and thoroughly realize the meaning of what Schelling so felicitously terms "the sublime indifference of Beauty." [3] Thus to enjoy with a keenly observant mind is the most dignified and salutary mode, and by no means the easiest one, of listening to music.

The most important factor in the mental process which accompanies the act of listening to music, and which converts it into a source of pleasure, is frequently overlooked. We here refer to the intellectual satisfaction which the listener derives from continually following and anticipating the composer's intentions—now to see his expectations fulfilled, and now to find himself agreeably mistaken. It is a matter of course that this intellectual flux and reflux, this perpetual giving and receiving, takes place unconsciously and with the rapidity of lightning flashes. Only that music can yield truly aesthetic enjoyment which prompts and rewards the act of thus closely following the composer's thoughts and which with perfect justice may be called a pondering of the imagination. Indeed, without mental activity no aesthetic enjoyment is possible. But the kind of mental activity alluded to is quite peculiar to music, because its products, instead of being fixed and presented to the mind at once in their completeness, develop gradually and thus do not permit the listener to linger at any point or to interrupt his train of thought. It demands, in fact, the keenest watching and the most untiring attention. In the case of intricate compositions, this may even become a mental exertion. Many an individual, nay, many a nation undertakes this exertion only with great reluctance. The monopoly of the soprano in the Italian school is mainly due to the mental indolence of the Italian people, who are incapable of that assiduous fixing of the attention so characteristic of northern races when listening to and enjoying a musical *chef d'oeuvre*, with all its intricacies of harmony and counterpoint. On the other hand, those whose store of mental energy is but small are more easily gratified, and such musical topers can consume quantities of music from which the aesthetic mind would shrink with dismay.

3 *Über das Verhältnis der bildenden Künste zur Natur.*

Mental activity is a necessary concomitant in every aesthetic enjoyment, and often varies very considerably in several individuals listening to one and the same composition. In the case of sensual and emotional natures it may sink to a minimum, whereas in highly intellectual persons it alone may turn the scale. It is the latter type of mind which in our opinion comes nearest to the "golden mean." To become intoxicated nothing but weakness is required, but truly aesthetic listening is an art in itself.[4]

The habit of reveling in sensation and emotion is generally limited to those who have not the preparatory knowledge for the aesthetic appreciation of musical beauty. With the technically uninitiated "the feelings" play a predominant part, while in the case of the trained musician these are quite in the background. The greater the aesthetic element in the listener's mind (just as in the work of art), the more it counterbalances purely sensuous influences. It is for this reason that the time-honored axiom of the theorists, "Grave music excites

[4] It is quite in keeping with W. Heinse's extravagant and dissolute nature to subordinate to a vague emotional impression the positive attributes of musical beauty. He goes so far (in *Hildegard von Hohenthal*) as to say: "True music . . . invariably aims at conveying to the listener the meaning of the words and the feelings they express, and it discharges this function so well and pleasantly that we are almost unconscious of it [the music]. Such music endures forever; it is so natural that we cease to be conscious of it as music, and only catch the meaning of the words."

The aesthetic appreciation of music, however, is only possible when our mind is fully awake; when we are "conscious" of the music and perfectly realize all its points of beauty. Heinse, to whose naturalism we must pay that tribute of admiration to which it is entitled, has been greatly overrated as a poet, and still more as a musician. In consequence of the paucity of original treatises on music, Heinse has gradually come to be regarded and quoted as one of the best writers on musical aesthetics. How could the fact ever be overlooked that, after a few appropriate remarks, there forthwith comes such a flood of platitudes and manifest errors as to make us marvel at so extraordinary an absence of culture? His want of technical knowledge is coupled with an unsound aesthetic judgment, of which his analyses of operas by Gluck, Jomelli, Traëtta, and others afford abundant proof. Instead of throwing any light on the subject of art, they contain scarcely anything but enthusiastic exclamations.

a feeling of sadness, and lively music makes us merry," is not always correct. If every shallow requiem, every noisy funeral march, and every whining adagio had the power to make us sad, who would care to prolong his existence in such a world? A composition that looks us in the face with the bright eyes of beauty would make us glad, though its object were to picture all the woes of the age; but the obstreperous gaiety of a finale by Verdi or a quadrille by Musard has not always had a cheering effect on us.

The untrained amateur and the musical sentimentalist are wont to ask whether the music is gay or mournful, whereas the instructed musician inquiries whether it is good or bad. The shadow cast by such questions plainly indicates the different positions in which the querists stand toward the source of light.

Although we assert that true aesthetic enjoyment depends upon the musical merit of the composition, it by no means follows that the simple call of a bugle or the sound of "yodeling" in the mountains may not at times afford us much greater delight than the most exquisite symphony. But in cases such as these music comes under the head of the unassisted charms of nature as distinguished from art. The impression is not produced by this particular combination of sounds but by this special kind of natural action, and in point of force it may, in conjunction with the rural beauty of the surroundings and the individual frame of mind, eclipse any aesthetic enjoyment whatsoever. The purely elemental may, therefore, preponderate over the artistic. Yet aesthetics, as the science of the beautiful in art, can judge music only in the sense of an art and can, therefore, take cognizance of nothing but those effects which, as products of the human mind, come within the scope of pure contemplation in consequence of the definite grouping of the primary factors.

Now the most essential condition to the aesthetic enjoyment of music is that of listening to a composition for its own sake, no matter what it is or what construction it may bear. The moment music is used as a means to induce certain states of mind, as accessory or ornamental, it ceases to be an art in a purely musical sense. The elemental properties of music are very frequently confounded with its artistic beauty; in other words, a part is taken for the whole, and unutterable confusion ensues. Hundreds of sayings about "music" do not apply to the art as such, but to the sensuous action of its material only.

When Shakespeare's Henry IV calls for music on his deathbed (Part II, Act IV), it is most assuredly not to listen attentively to the performance, but to lull himself with its ethereal elements, as in a dream. Nor are Portia and Bassanio (*Merchant of Venice*, Act III) likely to have greatly heeded the music which was being played during the ominous choosing of the casket. J. Strauss has composed charming, nay, highly original music for his waltzes, but it ceases to be such when it is used solely to beat time for the dancers. In all these cases it is utterly indifferent of what quality the music is, so long as it has the fundamental character needed for the occasion—and wherever the question of individuality is a matter of indifference we get a series of sounds, but no music. Only he who carries away with him, not simply the vague aftereffect of his feelings, but a definite and lasting impression of the particular composition, has truly heard and relished it. Those impressions which elevate our minds, and their supreme significance both in a psychical and a physiological sense, should not, however, hinder the art critic from distinguishing in any given effect between its sensuous and its aesthetic element. From an aesthetic point of view, music ought to be regarded as an effect rather than a cause, as a product rather than a producing agent.

Just as frequently as people confuse the elemental action of sound with music proper do they fail to distinguish the latter from the principles of rhythm and euphony, and from properties such as quiescence and motion, dissonance and consonance. The present state of music and philosophy forbids us, in the interest of both, to acquiesce in the expansion of the term "music" to the extent understood by the ancient Greeks, who used music in connection with all sciences and arts and the training of the mental faculties. The famous eulogy of music in *The Merchant of Venice* (Act V, Scene 1) [5] is the result of such a confusion of ideas, music itself being confounded with its principles of euphony, consonance, and rhythm. In aphorisms of this kind we may, without greatly altering the sense, substitute for "music" such words as "poetry," "art"—nay, "beauty." The preference over the other arts which music generally enjoys is due to its somewhat questionable attribute of popularity. Proof of this is to be found in the immediately preceding verses of the quoted passage, which are full of praise of the soothing effect which music has on animals, thus making it once again play the part of a Van Aken.

The most instructive examples are to be met with in Bettina's "musical explosions," as Goethe politely styled her letters on music. Bettina, as the genuine type of musical enthusiast, shows how improperly the meaning of the term "music" may be widened, in order to turn it freely to any use. Though ostensibly speaking of music, she always talks about the mysterious influence on her mind, and she willfully incapacitates herself for a dispassionate investigation by luxuriating in the dreams of a lively imagination. A musical composition she invariably regards as a kind of natural product, and not as a creation of the human mind. She, therefore, always understands music only in a purely phenomenological sense. The terms "music," "musical," Bettina applies to innumerable phenomena simply because they happen to have one attribute or another in common with music, such as euphony, rhythm, and the power of exciting emotions. The question, however, does not turn on these isolated factors, but on the specific mode in which they are combined, and through which they are elevated to the rank of an art. It is a matter of course that this romantic lady considers Goethe, nay, Christ himself,

[5] The man that has no music in himself,
   Nor is not moved with concord of sweet sounds,
   Is fit for treasons, stratagems, and spoils, . . .

as great musicians, though nobody knows whether the latter was one, and everybody knows that the former was not.

We respect historical modes of viewing things and the right of poetic license, and can quite understand why Aristophanes in his *Wasps* applies the epithets "wise and musical" (σοφὸν καὶ μουσικόν) to a highly cultured mind. Count Reinhardt's saying, too, that Oehlenschläger had "musical eyes" is very significant. In scientific inquiries, however, we must exclude from the term "music" any but its aesthetic meaning, unless we are to abandon all hope ever to establish this protean science on firm ground.

CHAPTER VI

MUSIC AND NATURE

To view a thing in its relation to nature is a proceeding of prime importance, and one likely to lead to most momentous results. Whoever has even slightly felt the pulse of the times knows that this conviction is rapidly gaining ground. In all modern research there is a strong leaning to study phenomena by the light of the laws of nature, so that inquiries even into the most abstruse subjects gravitate perceptibly toward the method obtaining in the natural sciences. The science of aesthetics, too, unless it be satisfied with a sort of sham existence, ought to know the knotty root as well as the delicate fiber by which every individual art is connected with the natural order of things. Now, the relation subsisting between music and nature discloses the most pregnant truths in respect of musical aesthetics, and on the just appreciation of this relation depends the treatment of its most difficult subjects and the solution of its most debatable points.

Art—considered, first of all, as passive, not as active—stands in a twofold relation to surrounding nature: primarily, in respect of the crude matter from which it produces; and secondly, in respect of the forms of beauty which the external world affords it for artistic reproduction. In both cases nature stands to art in the position of a kindly benefactress by supplying the most vital and essential requirements. It must now be our endeavor to quickly review these resources in the interest of musical aesthetics, and to inquire what share of the rational and, therefore, unequal gifts of nature has fallen to the lot of music.

On examining in what sense nature provides music with its material, we find that she supplies nothing but the rough elements, from which man contrives to elicit sounds. The silent ore of the mountains, the wood of the forest, the skin and gut of animals, are all that constitute the raw material, properly so-called, with which the musical note is formed. At the outset, therefore, we are furnished only with material for the production of material, that is, of sound of high or low pitch; in other words, the measurable tone. The latter is the primary and essential condition of all music, whose function it is to so combine these tones as to produce melody and harmony, its two main factors. Neither of them is provided for us by nature ready-made, but both are creations of the human mind.

The systematic succession of measurable tones which we call "melody" is not to be met with in nature, even in its most rudimentary form. Sound phenomena in unassisted nature present no intelligible proportions, nor can they be reduced to our scale. Melody, on the other hand, is the "initial force," the lifeblood, the primitive cell of the musical organism, with which the drift and development of the composition are closely bound up.

Just as little as melody do we find in nature—the sublime harmony of its phenomena notwithstanding—harmony in a musical sense, the simultaneous occurrence of certain notes. Has anybody ever heard a triad, a chord of the sixth or the seventh in nature? Harmony, like melody, is an achievement of man, only belonging to a much later period.

The Greeks knew of no harmony, but sang in octaves or in unison, just as do at the present time those Asiatic tribes who are known to sing. The use of dissonances (among which we must include the third and the sixth) came gradually into vogue in the twelfth century, while as late as the fifteenth century, to effect modulations, the octave only was used. All the intervals which our present system of harmony puts into requisition had to be discovered one by one, and often more than a century was needed for so insignificant an acquisition. Neither the race that most cultivated art in ancient times nor the most erudite composers of the early part of the Middle Ages were able to do what our shepherdesses of the most out-of-the-way mountains can do at the present day—to sing in thirds. It must not be supposed, however, that the introduction of harmony was an additional source of light to music, for it was through harmony that the art first emerged from utter darkness. "Music, properly so called, was not born until then" (Nägeli).

We have seen that nature is destitute both of melody and harmony; but there is a third factor regulating the two former, which existed prior to man and is consequently not of his creation. This factor is rhythm. In the galloping of the horse, the clack of the mill, the singing of the blackbird and the quail, there is an element of periodically recurring motion in the successive beats which, when looked at in the aggregate, blend into an intelligible whole. Not all, yet many sounds in nature are rhythmical, and in these the principle of duple-time rhythm (manifesting itself in the rise and fall, the ebb and flow) is invariably discernible. But the point in which natural rhythm differs from human music is obvious: in music there is no independent rhythm; it occurs only in connection with melody and harmony expressed in rhythmical order. Rhythm in nature, on the other hand, is associated neither with melody nor harmony, but is perceptible only in aerial vibrations that cannot be reduced to a definite quantity. It is the only musical element which nature possesses, the first we are conscious of, and that with which the mind of the infant and the savage becomes soonest familiar. When South Sea islanders rattle wooden staves and pieces of metal to the accompaniment of fearful howlings, they are performing natural music, that is, no music at all. But what a Tyrolese peasant sings, though apparently uninfluenced by art culture, is, beyond dispute, artificial music. The man fancies, of course, that he sings as nature prompts him, but to enable nature so to prompt him the seed of centuries had to grow and ripen.

We have now examined the elements which form the groundwork of the music of today, and have been forced to the conclusion that man has not learned it from surrounding nature. The manner and sequence in which music developed into our present system is a subject treated in the history of music. Here it is enough to take the facts for granted and to emphasize the conclusions arrived at—namely, that melody and harmony, our intervals and our scale, the divisions into major and minor according to the position of the semitone, and lastly, the equal temperament without which our music (the West European) would be impossible, are slowly gained triumphs of the human mind. Nature has given man but the organs and the inclination to sing, together with the faculty to create a musical system having its roots in the most simple relations of sound. Only the latter (the triad, harmonic progression) will ever remain the indestructible foundation upon which all future development must rest. Let us keep clear of the error that this (the present) musical system is itself an inherent element in nature. Although even scientists nowadays manipulate musical relations, to all appearance, without any difficulty, as though the power to do so were innate, this by no means proves our present musical laws to be so many laws of nature, but is simply due to the enormous spread of musical culture. Hand, therefore, is quite right in remarking that our infants in the cradle sing better than adult savages. "If the succession of musical notes were a necessary product of nature, everybody would sing in tune." [1]

If we apply the term "artificial" to our musical system, it must not be construed into the subtilized meaning of an arbitrary and conventional arrangement, but as signifying something that has gradually developed, as distinguished from something pre-existing in a complete form.

Hauptmann overlooks this distinction when he calls the

[1] Hand (*Aesthetik der Tonkunst,* I, 50) also very justly directs attention to the fact that the musical scales of the Scottish Gaels and the various tribes of India are alike in the peculiarity of having neither fourth nor seventh, the succession of their notes being C, D, E, G, A, C. The physically well-developed Patagonians in South America are entirely ignorant of both vocal and instrumental music. Our above conclusions, moreover, are amply confirmed by the recent and exhaustive inquiries of Helmholtz into the growth of our present system of music (*Lehre von den Tonempfindungen*).

notion of an artificial system of music an "absolutely empty one, because musicians were just as powerless to devise intervals and a musical system as philologists to invent the words and the construction of a language." [2] Language is an artificial product in precisely the same sense as music, since neither exists ready prepared in nature, but both have been formed by degrees and have to be specially learned. Languages are not framed by philologists but by the nations themselves according to their idiosyncrasies, and, by way of perfecting them, modifications are continually introduced. In the same way "musical philologists" have not laid the "foundation" of music, but have merely fixed and substantiated what generations of musical talents have unconsciously brought forth with rational consistency, though not with inherent necessity.[3] From this process of evolution we may infer that our musical system will also, in the course of time, be enriched with new forms and undergo further changes. Music within its present limits, however, is still capable of such great development that an alteration in the nature of the system seems a very remote contingency as yet. If, for instance, the system were widened by the "emancipation of the demisemitones" (of which a modern authoress professes to have found adumbrations in Chopin's music),[4] the theories of harmony, composition, and musical aesthetics would become totally changed. The musical theorist may, therefore, at present, indulge in this glimpse into the future only so far as to concede the bare possibility of such changes.

To disprove our assertion that there is no music in nature, the wealth of sound that enlivens her is generally cited as counterevidence. Should not the murmuring brook, the roar of the ocean waves, the thundering avalanche, and the howl-

2 M. Hauptmann, *Die Natur der Harmonik und Metrik* (1853), p. 7.

3 Our view accords with the researches of Jacob Grimm, who among other things remarks, "Whoever has gained the conviction that language has originated in the alembic of the human mind will have no doubt as to the source of poetry and music" (*Ursprung der Sprache*, 1852).

4 Johanna Kinkel, *Acht Briefe über Clavierunterricht* (Cotta, 1852).

ing of the wind be at once the source of and the model for human music? Have all these rippling, whistling, and roaring noises nothing to do with our system of music? We have no option but to reply in the negative. All such sounds are mere noise, i.e., an irregular succession of sonorous pulses. Very seldom, and even then only in an isolated manner, does nature bring forth a musical note of definite and measurable pitch. But a musical note is the foundation of all music. However deeply and agreeably these natural sounds may affect the mind, they form no steppingstones to human music but are mere elemental semblances of it; though it is true that eventually they may, for the mature human music, become highly suggestive factors. Even the purest phenomenon in the natural world of sound—the song of birds—has no relation to music, as it cannot be reduced to our scale. Natural harmony, too—certainly the sole and indestructible basis existing in nature, on which the principal relations of our music repose—should be viewed in its true light. Harmonic progression on the Aeolian harp (an instrument with all its strings alike) is produced by the spontaneous action of nature, and is grounded, therefore, on some natural law; but the progression itself is not the immediate product of nature. Unless a certain measurable, fundamental tone be sounded on a musical instrument, there can be no auxiliary tones and consequently no harmonic progression. Man must ask before nature can reply. The reflection of sound, called echo, is susceptible of a still simpler explanation. It is a singular fact that even authors of great ability fail to recognize the fallacy that there is real music in nature. Hand himself (whom we have intentionally quoted before to testify to his accurate judgment respecting the incommensurableness and the inapplicability of natural sounds for purposes of art) devotes a special chapter to "Music in Nature," of which the sonorous waves might "in a manner" also be called music. Krüger expresses himself similarly.[5] But when it is a question of first principles, saving clauses such as

[5] *Beiträge für Leben und Wissenschaft der Tonkunst*, p. 149, etc.

"in a manner" are wholly inadmissible: the sounds we hear in nature either are, or are not, music. The criterion can only be the measurableness of the tone. Hand continually emphasizes "the inspiration," "the revealing of the inner man" and of a "subjective feeling," "the force of individual energy, through which the inmost thoughts find direct utterance." According to this principle the singing of birds ought to be called music, whereas the tune of a music box ought not to be called so. Yet the very opposite is the truth.

The "music" of nature and the music of man belong to two distinct categories. The transition from the former to the latter passes through the science of mathematics. An important and pregnant proposition. Still, we should be wrong were we to construe it in the sense that man framed his musical system according to calculations purposely made, the system having arisen through the unconscious application of pre-existent conceptions of quantity and proportion, through subtle processes of measuring and counting; but the laws by which the latter are governed were demonstrated only subsequently by science.

As everything in music must be measurable, while the spontaneous sounds of nature cannot be reduced to any definite quantity, these two realms of sound have no true point of contact. Nature does not supply us with the art elements of a complete and ready-prepared system of sound, but only with the crude matter which we utilize for our music. Not the voices of animals but their gut is of importance to us; and the animal to which music is most indebted is not the nightingale but the sheep.

After this preliminary inquiry, which for the just appreciation of the musically beautiful is but the basement, indispensable though it be, we will pass onward to a higher region, to the domain of aesthetics.

The measurable tone and the complete system are merely the means with which the composer produces, not what he produces. As wood and ore are but "matter" in respect of the tone, so the tone is but "matter" in respect of music. But there is a third and higher sense of the term "matter": matter in the sense of the subject to be treated—the idea to be conveyed—the theme. Whence does the composer derive the matter thus understood? Whence arise the contents of any given composition, the subject which gives it its individual and distinctive character?

Poetry, painting, and sculpture possess in surrounding nature an inexhaustible store of subject matter. The poet or artist here is impressed by some beautiful object in nature which forthwith becomes the subject of some original production.

The function of nature to supply art with models is most strikingly exemplified in painting and sculpture. The painter could draw no tree, no flower, if they did not already exist in the external world; the sculptor could produce no statue without knowing the human form, and without using it as a model. The same holds good of ideal subjects. In the strict sense of the word they are not "ideal." Is not the "ideal" landscape composed of rocks, trees, water, drifts of cloud—of things, in brief, which occur in nature? The painter can paint nothing but what he has seen and closely observed, no matter whether he paints a landscape, a "genre" or a historical painting. When our contemporaries paint "Huss," "Luther," or "Egmont," though they have never actually beheld their subject, its component parts cannot have been copied but from nature. The painter need not necessarily have seen this very man, but he must have seen a great number of men moving, standing, and walking; he must have noticed their appearance when illuminated or when casting shadows. The impossibility or unreality of the painter's figures would assuredly be his greatest reproach.

Poetry, which nature furnishes with a far wider range of beautiful models, is in an analogous position. Man and his deeds, his feelings and sufferings, as coming under our own observation or as handed down to us by tradition—for tradition, too, is a pre-existing factor, something which the poet finds already supplied—are the subject matter of the poem, the tragedy, the novel. The poet can give us no description of a sunrise, a snow field, or an emotion; he can introduce neither peasant, soldier, miser, nor lover into his play without having seen or studied their originals in nature, or without being enabled by accurate accounts to form in his own mind such vivid images of them as compensate for the want of having them actually present.

Now, on comparing music with those arts, it is obvious that nature has provided no model capable of becoming its subject matter.

There is nothing beautiful in nature as far as music is concerned.

This distinction between music and the other arts (with the sole exception of architecture, which is likewise without models in nature) is a profound and momentous one.

The work of the painter or poet is a continual copying or reproducing (drawn from reality or the imagination), but it is impossible to copy music from nature. Nature knows of no sonata, no overture, no rondo; but she knows of landscapes, of scenes of everyday life, of idyls and tragedies. The Aristotelian proposition that it is the office of art to imitate nature —a proposition which philosophers even of the last century viewed with favor—has long since been amended, and, having been commented upon *ad nauseam,* it needs no further exposition in this inquiry. Art should not slavishly copy nature but remodel it. This expression alone shows that something must have existed prior to art that admits of being remodeled. This something is the prototype, the thing of beauty which nature provides for art. A beautiful landscape, a group, or a poem inspires the painter to an artistic reproduction, while the poet is similarly inspired by a historical event or by some adventure. But what is there in nature that could ever induce the composer to exclaim: What a magnificent model for an overture, a symphony! The composer can remodel nothing; he has to create everything *ab initio.* That which the painter or the poet gleans in contemplating the beautiful in nature, the composer has to draw from his own fertile imagination. He

must watch for the propitious moment when it begins to ring
and sing within him; he will then enter heart and soul into
his task and create from within that which has not its like in
nature and which, therefore, unlike the other arts, is truly not
of this world.

If, in respect of the painter and the poet, we classed man
with the "beautiful objects" in nature, whereas in respect of
the composer we excluded the rich melodies of man in their
pristine freshness, we did not do so from bias. The singing
shepherd is not an object but a subject of our art. His song,
if consisting of measurable and systematically adjusted successions of notes, how simple soever these may be, is a creation of
the human mind, no matter whether a herdboy or a Beethoven
invented it.

A composer who introduces into his music true national airs
does not thereby make use of a spontaneous product of nature,
the airs being always traceable to someone who originated
them. How did he come by them? Did he copy them from a
model in nature? This is the question we must ask, and only a
negative reply is possible. Popular airs are not things already
existing—natural objects of beauty, as it were—but they are the
first stage of true art, art in its native simplicity. Such airs are
natural models for music just as little as the flowers and
soldiers daubed with charcoal on the walls of guardrooms and
lumberyards are natural models for painting. Both are products of human art. Of the figures drawn in charcoal the
originals exist in nature, whereas for the popular air no such
original exists; it cannot be traced to any prototype in nature.

A very common error arises from the term "subject" being
understood in its wider sense when speaking of music, in
support of which it is pointed out that Beethoven really composed an overture to *Egmont* or (to avoid reminding us by the
preposition "to" of its dramatic meaning) that Beethoven
composed *Egmont*, Berlioz *King Lear,* and Mendelssohn
Melusina. Have not these narratives, say they, furnished the
composer with subjects as they do the poet? Not in the least.
To the poet these characters are true models which he recasts,

whereas to the composer they are mere suggestions, i.e., poetic suggestions. The natural model for the composer would have to be an audible something, as it is a visible something for the painter and a tangible something for the sculptor. The individuality of Egmont, his deeds, experiences, and sentiments, do not form the subject of Beethoven's overture, as they do in the case of the painting or the drama *Egmont*. The subject of the overture consists of successions of notes which the composer drew from the store of his own imagination, free from all limitations except those fixed by the intrinsic laws of music. These successions of notes are, aesthetically speaking, entirely independent of the idea "Egmont" with which the poetic fancy of the composer alone has linked them; no matter whether this idea first suggested them in some inscrutable manner or whether he subsequently found them suitable for his composition. This connection, however, is so loose and arbitrary that in listening to a piece of music we should never even guess at its alleged subject but for the name purposely attached to it by the author. It is this name alone which, from the very beginning, forces our thoughts into a certain channel. Berlioz' magnificent overture is no more causally related to the idea "King Lear" than a waltz by Strauss. It is impossible to lay too much stress upon this fact, as the most erroneous ideas prevail on this very point. Only on comparing the waltz by Strauss or the overture by Berlioz with the idea "King Lear" does the former appear to be inconsistent and the latter consistent with it. But we are induced to make the comparison by the explicit command of the author, and not by something inherent in the music itself. A certain title prompts us to contrast the piece of music with some object external to it, and we are thus under the necessity of measuring it by some standard other than the musical one.

It may possibly be said that Beethoven's overture to *Prometheus* is not sufficiently grand for the subject, but intrinsically it is proof against all attacks and nowhere can a musical flaw or imperfection be shown to exist. The overture is perfect because the working out of its *musical* subject is faultless. To treat its *poetic* part in like manner is a totally different matter. The poetic treatment arises and disappears with the title. In the case of a composition with a definite title, this demand can, moreover, only apply to certain characteristic attributes: the music may have to be solemn or lively, gloomy or cheerful; its opening may have to be simple and its close gay or mournful, etc. Poetry and painting are expected to clothe their subjects in a definite and concrete individuality, and not merely with general attributes. For this reason it is quite conceivable that Beethoven's overture to *Egmont* would bear equally well the title "William Tell" or "Joan of Arc." But the drama *Egmont* or the painting "Egmont" could at worst only lead to the error that another individual in the same position is meant but not that the circumstances themselves are entirely different.

It is clear, therefore, that the relation of music to nature is most intimately connected with the question of its subject matter.

There is still another factor selected from musical literature for the purpose of proving that music has a prototype in nature. Instances are adduced of composers having derived from nature not only their poetic inspiration (as in the cases alluded to), but of having faithfully reproduced some of her spontaneous utterances: the cockcrowing in Haydn's oratorio, *The Seasons;* the call of the cuckoo, the song of the nightingale, the whistle of the quail in Beethoven's *Pastoral Symphony* and in Spohr's *Consecration of Sound.* But though we recognize these imitations, and though we listen to them in a musical work, their meaning is a poetic and not a musical one. The cockcrowing is not introduced as beautiful music, or indeed as music at all, but merely to recall in us the impression associated in our mind with the phenomenon in question. "I have almost *seen* Haydn's *Creation,*" wrote Thieriot to Jean Paul, after listening to a performance of this oratorio. We are only reminded by universally known sayings and quotations that it is early morn, a balmy summer's night, or springtime. Except in a purely descriptive sense, no composer has ever been able to utilize the sounds of nature for any truly musical purpose. All the natural sounds in the world are powerless to produce a single musical theme, simply because they are not music, and it is significant that music can only enlist nature into its service if it wants to dabble in the art of painting.[6]

[6] The misconception that the spontaneous sounds of nature should be bodily transferred to a musical composition—which, as O. Jahn aptly remarks, is admissible only in rare cases as a jest—is a totally different thing from such cases (which, by the way, ought not to be called "painting" at all) where semimusical phenomena, through their rhythmic or sonorous character, e.g., the rushing and splashing of water, the singing of birds, the howling of the wind, the whizzing of arrows, the humming of the spinning wheel, etc., suggest to the composer—but are by no means "literally copied" by him—themes of independent beauty, which are worked out with perfect freedom and bear the impress of true art. "Of this privilege the poet makes use in the choice of the words and the meter; but in music it extends over a much wider area, countless musical elements being scattered throughout nature." An abundance of notable examples is supplied both by classical and modern composers; only the latter proceed with much greater subtlety than did the former.

CHAPTER VII

THE SUBJECT OF MUSIC

Has music any subject? This has been a burning question ever since people began to reflect upon music. It has been answered both in the affirmative and in the negative. Many prominent men, almost exclusively philosophers, among whom we may mention Rousseau, Kant, Hegel, Herbart,[1] Kahlert, etc., hold that music has no subject. The numerous physiologists who endorse this view include such eminent thinkers as Lotze and Helmholtz, whose opinions, strengthened as they are by musical knowledge, carry great weight and authority. Those who contend that music has a subject are numerically far stronger: among them are the trained musicians of the literary profession, and their convictions are shared by the bulk of the public.

It may seem almost a matter for surprise that just those who are familiar with the technical side of music should be unwilling to concede the untenableness of a doctrine which is at variance with those very technical principles and which thinkers on abstract subjects might perhaps be pardoned for propounding. The reason is that many of these musical authors are more anxious to save the so-called honor of their art than to ascertain the truth. They attack the doctrine that music has no subject, not as one opinion against another, but as heresy against dogma. The contrary view appears to them in the light of a degrading error and a form of crude and heinous materialism. "What! the art that charms and elevates us, to which so many noble minds have devoted a whole life-

---

[1] Robert Zimmermann, in his recent work, *Die allgemeine Aesthetik als Formwissenschaft* (Vienna, 1865), founded as it is on Herbart's principles, has applied the morphological principle with strict logical consistency to all arts, and consequently also to music.

time, which is the vehicle of the most sublime thoughts—*that* art to be cursed with unmeaningness, to be mere food for the senses, mere empty sound!" Hackneyed exclamations of this description, which, though made up of several disconnected propositions, are generally uttered in one breath, neither prove nor disprove anything. The question is not a point of honor, not a party badge, but simply the discovery of truth; and in order to attain this object, it is of the first importance to be clear regarding the points which are under debate.

It is the indiscriminate use of the terms "contents," "subject," "matter," which has been, and still is, responsible for all this ambiguity; the same meaning being expressed by different terms, or the same term associated with different meanings. "Contents," in the true and original sense, is that which a thing contains, what it holds within. The notes of which a piece of music is composed, and which are the parts that go to make up the whole, are the contents in this sense. The circumstance that nobody will accept this definition as a satisfactory solution but that it is dismissed as a truism is due to the word "contents" (subject) being usually confounded with the word "object." An inquiry into the "contents" of musical compositions raises in such people's minds the conception of an "object" (subject matter, topic), which latter, being the idea, the ideal element, they represent to themselves as almost antithetical to the "material part," the musical notes. Music has, indeed, no contents as thus understood; no subject in the sense that the subject to be treated is something extraneous to the musical notes. Kahlert is right in emphatically maintaining that music, unlike painting, admits of no "description in words" (*Aesthetik*, p. 380), though his subsequent assumption that a description in words may, at times, "compensate for the want of aesthetic enjoyment" is false. It may be the means, however, of clearly perceiving the real bearing of the question. The query, What is the subject of the music? must necessarily be answerable in words if music really has a "subject," because an "indefinite subject" upon which everyone puts a different construction, which can only be felt

and not translated into words, is not a subject as we have
defined it.

Music consists of successions and forms of sound, and these
alone constitute the subject. They again remind us of architecture and dancing, which likewise aim at beauty in form
and motion and are also devoid of a definite subject. Now,
whatever be the effect of a piece of music on the individual
mind, and howsoever it be interpreted, it has no subject
beyond the combinations of notes we hear, for music speaks
not only by means of sounds, it speaks nothing but sound.

Krüger—the opponent of Hegel and Kahlert, who is probably the most learned advocate of the doctrine that music has
a "subject"—contends that this art presents but a different side
of the subject which other arts, such as painting, represent.
"All plastic figures," he says (Beiträge, p. 131), "are in a state
of quiescence; they do not exhibit present, but past, action, or
the state of things at a given moment. The painting, therefore, does not show Apollo vanquishing, but it represents the
victor, the furious warrior," etc. Music, on the other hand,
"supplies to those plastic and quiescent forms the motive
force, the active principle, the inner waves of motion; and
whereas in the former instance we knew the true but inert
subject to be anger, love, etc., we here know the true and
active subject to be loving, rushing, heaving, storming, fum-
ing." The latter portion is only partly true, for though music
may be said to "rush, heave, and storm," it can neither "love"
nor be "angry." These sentiments we ourselves import into
the music, and we must here refer our readers to the second
chapter of this book. Krüger then proceeds to compare the
definiteness of the painter's subject with the musical subject,
and remarks: "The painter represents Orestes, pursued by the
Furies: his outward appearance, his eyes, mouth, forehead,
and posture, give us the impression of flight, gloom, and
despair; at his heels the spirits of divine vengeance, whose
imperious and sublimely terrible commands he cannot evade
but who likewise present unchanging outlines, features, and
attitudes. The composer does not exhibit fleeing Orestes in

fixed lines but from a point of view from which the painter cannot portray him: he puts into his music the tremor and shuddering of his soul, his inmost feelings at war, urging his flight," etc. This, in our opinion, is entirely false; the composer is unable to represent Orestes either in one way or another; in fact, he cannot represent him at all.

The objection that sculpture and painting are also unable to represent to us a given historical personage, and that we could not know the figure to be this very individual but for our previous knowledge of certain historical facts, does not hold good. True, the figure does not proclaim itself to be Orestes, the man who has gone through such or such experiences and whose existence is bound up with certain biographic incidents (none but the poet can represent that, since he alone can narrate the events); but the painting "Orestes" unequivocally shows us a youth with noble features, in Greek attire, his looks and attitude betokening fear and mental anguish—and it shows us this youth pursued and tormented by the awe-inspiring goddesses of vengeance. All this is clear and indubitable, a visible narrative—no matter whether the youth be called Orestes or otherwise. Only the antecedent causes, namely, that the youth has committed matricide, etc., cannot be expressed. Now, what can music give us in point of definiteness as a counterpart to the visible subject of the painter—apart from the historical element? Chords of a diminished seventh, themes in minor keys, a rolling bass, etc. —musical forms, in brief, which might signify a woman just as well as a youth; one pursued by Myrmidons instead of Furies; somebody tortured by jealousy or by bodily pain; one bent on revenge—in short, anything we can think of, if we must needs imagine a subject for the composition.

It seems almost superfluous to recall expressly the proposition, already established by us, that whenever the subject and the descriptive power of music are under debate, instrumental music alone can be taken into account. Nobody is likely to disregard this so far as to instance Orestes in Gluck's *Iphigenia,* for this Orestes is not the composer's creation. The words of the poet, the appearance and gestures of the actor, the costume and the painter's decorations produce the complete Orestes. The composer's contribution—the melody—is possibly the most beautiful part of all, but it happens to be just that factor which has nothing whatever to do with the real Orestes.

Lessing has shown with admirable perspicuity what the poet and what the sculptor or painter may make of the story of Laocoön. The poet by the aid of speech gives us the historical, individually defined Laocoön; the painter and sculptor show us the terrible serpents, crushing in their coils an old man and two boys (of determinate age and appearance, dressed after a particular fashion, etc.), who by their looks, attitudes, and gestures express the agonies of approaching death. Of the composer, Lessing says nothing, and this was only to be expected since there is nothing in "Laocoön" which could be turned into music.

We have already alluded to the intimate connection between the question of subject in musical compositions and the relation of music to the beauties of nature. The composer looks in vain for models such as those which render the subjects of other art products both definite and recognizable, and an art for which nature can provide no aesthetic model must, properly speaking, be incorporeal. A prototype of its mode of manifestation is nowhere to be met with, and it cannot, therefore, be included in the range of living experiences. It does not reproduce an already known and classified subject, and for this reason it has no subject that can be taken hold of by the intellect, as the latter can be exercised only on definite conceptions.

The term "subject" (substance) can, properly speaking, be applied to an art product only if we regard it as the correlative of "form." The terms "form" and "substance" supplement each other, and one cannot be thought of except in relation to the other. Wherever the "form" appears mentally inseparable from the "substance" there can be no question of an independent "substance" (subject). Now in music, substance and form, the subject and its working out, the image and the realized conception, are mysteriously blended in one undecomposable whole. This complete fusion of substance and form is exclusively characteristic of music, and presents a sharp contrast to poetry, painting, and sculpture, inasmuch as these arts are capable of representing the same idea and the same event in different forms. The story of William Tell supplied to Florian the subject for a historical novel, to Schiller the subject for a play, while Goethe began to treat it as an epic poem. The substance is everywhere the same, equally resolvable into prose, and capable of being narrated; always clearly recognizable, and yet the form differs in each case. Aphrodite emerging from the sea is the subject of innumerable paintings and statues, the various forms of which it is nevertheless impossible to confuse. In music no distinction can be made between substance and form, as it has no form independent of the substance. Let us look at this more closely.

In all compositions the independent, aesthetically undecomposable subject of a musical conception is the theme, and by the theme, the musical microcosm, we should always be able to test the alleged subject underlying the music as such. Let us examine the leading theme of some composition, say that of Beethoven's symphony in B flat major. What is its subject (substance)? What its form? Where does the latter commence and the former end? That its subject does not consist of a determinate feeling we think we have conclusively proved, and this truth becomes only the more evident when tested by this or by any other concrete example. What then is to be called its subject? The groups of sounds? Undoubtedly; but they have a form already. And what is the form? The groups of sounds again; but here they are a replete form. Every practical attempt at resolving a theme into subject and form ends in arbitrariness and contradiction. Take, for instance, a theme repeated by another instrument or in the higher octave. Is the subject changed thereby or the form? If, as is generally the case, the latter is said to be changed, then all that remains as the subject of the theme would simply be the series of intervals, the skeleton frame for the musical notations as the score presents them to the eye. But this is not musical definiteness; it is an abstract notion. It may be likened to a pavilion with stained windowpanes through which the same environment appears now red, now blue, and now yellow. The environment itself changes neither in substance nor in form, but merely in color. This property of exhibiting the same forms in countless hues, from the most glaring contrasts down to the finest distinctions of shade, is quite peculiar to music and is one of the most fertile and powerful causes of its effectiveness.

A theme originally composed for the piano and subsequently arranged for the orchestra acquires thereby a new form but not a form for the first time, the formal element being part and parcel of the primary conception. The assertion that a theme by the process of instrumentation changes its subject while retaining its form is even less tenable, as such a theory involves still greater contradictions, the listener being obliged to affirm that though he recognizes it to be the same subject "it somehow sounds like a different one."

It is true that in looking at a composition in the aggregate, and more particularly at musical works of great length, we are in the habit of speaking of form and subject; in such a case, however, these terms are not understood in their primitive and logical sense, but in a specifically musical one. What we call the "form" of a symphony, an overture, a sonata, an aria, a chorus, etc., is the architectonic combination of the units and groups of units of which a composition is made up; or, more definitely speaking, the symmetry of their successions, their contrasts, repetitions, and general working out. But thus understood, the subject is identical with the themes with which this architectonic structure is built up. Subject is here, therefore, no longer construed in the sense of an "object," but as the subject in a purely musical sense. The words "substance" and "form" in respect of entire compositions are used in an aesthetic and not in a strictly logical sense. If we wish to apply them to music in the latter sense we must do so, not in relation to the composition in the aggregate, as a whole consisting of parts, but in relation to its ultimate and aesthetically undecomposable idea. This ultimate idea is the theme or themes, and, in the latter, substance and form are indissolubly connected. We cannot acquaint anybody with the "subject" of a theme except by playing it. The subject of a composition cannot, therefore, be understood as an object derived from an external source, but as something intrinsically musical; in other words, as the concrete group of sounds in a piece of music. Now, as a composition must comply with the formal laws of beauty, it cannot run on arbitrarily and at random, but must develop gradually with intelligible and organic definiteness, as buds develop into rich blossoms.

Here we have the principal theme, the true topic or subject of the entire composition. Everything it contains, though originated by the unfettered imagination, is nevertheless the natural outcome and effect of the theme which determines and forms, regulates and pervades its every part. We may compare it to a self-evident truth which we accept for a moment as satisfactory but which our mind would fain see tested and developed, and in the musical working out this development takes place analogously to the logical train of reasoning in an argument. The theme, not unlike the chief hero in a novel, is brought by the composer into the most varied states and surrounding conditions, and is made to pass through ever-changing phases and moods—everything, no matter what contrasts it may present, is conceived and formed in relation to the theme.

The epithet "without a subject" might possibly be applied to the freest form of extemporizing, during which the performer indulges in chords, arpeggios, and rosalias by way of a rest, rather than as a creative effort, and which does not end in the production of a definite and connected whole. Such extempore playing has no individuality of its own by which one might recognize or distinguish it, and it would be quite correct to say that it has no subject (in the wider sense of the term) because it has no theme.

Thus the theme or the themes are the real subject of a piece of music.

In aesthetic and critical reviews, far too little importance is attached to the leading theme of a composition; it alone reveals at once the mind which conceived the work. Every musician, on hearing the first few opening bars of Beethoven's overture to *Leonore* or Mendelssohn's overture to *The Hebrides,* though he may be totally unaware of the subsequent development of the theme, must recognize at once the treasure that lies before him; whereas the music of a theme from Donizetti's *Fausta* overture or Verdi's overture to *Louisa Miller* will, without the need of further examination, convince us that the music is fit only for low music halls. German theorists and executants prize the musical working-out far more than the inherent merits of the theme. But whatever is not contained in the theme (be it overtly or in disguise) is incapable of organic growth, and if the present time is barren of orchestral works of the Beethoven type it is, perhaps, due not so much to an imperfect knowledge of the working out, as to the want of symphonic power and fertility of the themes.

On inquiring into the subject of music we should, above all, beware of using the term "subject" in a eulogistic sense. From the fact that music has no extrinsic subject (object) it does not follow that it is without any intrinsic merit. It is clear that those who, with the zeal of partisanship, contend that music has a "subject" really mean "intellectual merit." We can only ask our readers to revert to our remarks in the third chapter of this book. Music is to be played, but it is not to be played with. Thoughts and feelings pervade with vital energy the musical organism, the embodiment of beauty and symmetry, and though they are not identical with the organism itself nor yet visible, they are, as it were, its breath of life. The composer thinks and works; but he thinks and works in sound, away from the realities of the external world. We deliberately repeat this commonplace, for even those who admit it in principle deny and violate it when carried to its logical conclusions. They conceive the act of composing as a translation into sound of a given subject, whereas the sounds themselves are the untranslatable and original tongue. If the composer is obliged to think in sounds, it follows as a matter of course that music has no subject external to itself, for of a subject in this sense we ought to be able to think in words.

Though, when examining into the subject of music, we rigorously excluded compositions written for given sets of words as being inconsistent with the conception of music pure and simple, yet the masterpieces of vocal music are indispensable for the formation of an accurate judgment respecting the intrinsic worth of music. From the simple song to the complex opera and the time-honored practice of using music for the celebration of religious services, music has never ceased to accompany the most tender and profound affections of the human mind, and has thus been the indirect means of glorifying them.

Apart from the existence of an intrinsic merit, there is a second corollary which we wish to emphasize. Though music possesses beauty of form without any extrinsic subject, this does not deprive it of the quality of individuality. The act of inventing a certain theme and the mode of working it out are always so unique and specific as to defy their inclusion in a wider generality. These processes are distinctly and unequivocally individual in nature. A theme of Mozart or Beethoven rests on as firm and independent a foundation as a poem by Goethe, an epigram by Lessing, a statue by Thorvaldsen, or a painting by Overbeck. The independent musical thoughts (themes) possess the identity of a quotation and the distinctness of a painting; they are individual, personal, eternal.

Unable as we were to endorse Hegel's opinion respecting the want of intellectual merit in music, it seems to us a still more glaring error on his part to assert that the sole function of music is the expressing of an "inner nonindividuality." Even from Hegel's musical point of view, which, while overlooking the inherently form-giving and objective activity of the composer, conceives music as the free manifestation of purely subjective states, its want of individuality by no means follows, since the subjectively producing mind is essentially individual.

How the individuality shows itself in the choice and working out of the various musical elements we have already pointed out in the third chapter. The stigma that music has no subject is, therefore, quite unmerited. Music has a subject, i.e., a musical subject, which is no less a vital spark of the divine fire than the beautiful of any other art. Yet only by steadfastly denying the existence of any other "subject" in music is it possible to save its "true subject." The indefinite emotions which at best underlie the other kind of subject do not explain its spiritual force. The latter can only be attributed to the definite beauty of musical form as the result of the untrammeled working of the human mind on material susceptible of intellectual manipulation.